Vasco Núñez de Balboa

THE WORLD'S GREAT EXPLORERS

Vasco Núñez de Balboa

By Maureen Ash

CHILDRENS PRESS ®

CHICAGO

Statue of Balboa in Panama City, Panama

Project Editor: Ann Heinrichs
Designer: Lindaanne Donohoe
Cover Art: Steven Gaston Dobson
Engraver: Liberty Photoengraving

**Library of Congress
Cataloging-in-Publication Data**

Ash, Maureen.
  Vasco Núñez de Balboa / by Maureen Ash.
    p. cm. — (The World's great explorers)
  Includes bibliographical references and index.
  Summary: Traces the life of the Spanish explorer, focusing on his discovery of the Pacific Ocean.
    ISBN 0-516-03057-4
  1. Balboa, Vasco Núñez de, 1475-1519— Juvenile literature. 2. Explorers—America—Biography—Juvenile literature. 3. Explorers—Spain—Biography—Juvenile literature. 4. America—Discovery and exploration—Spanish—Juvenile literature. [1. Balboa, Vasco Núñez de, 1475-1519. 2. Explorers. 3. America—Discovery and exploration—Spanish.] I. Title. II. Series.
E125.B2A85 1990
973.1'6'092—dc20   90-2230
[B]   CIP
[92]   AC

Balboa's discovery of the Pacific Ocean from a peak in Darién

Table of Contents

Chapter 1
The Fight to the Ocean

One day nearly five hundred years ago, a group of one hundred fifty Spanish soldiers stood at the top of a hill. They checked and re-checked their swords, crossbows, and arquebuses, a sort of primitive rifle. Their dogs, specially trained to fight, strained to be unleashed. The Spaniards faced an army of one thousand Indian warriors from the village of Quareca.

The warriors were confident that they would defeat the ragged band of Spanish men. Hadn't they won every battle they'd ever fought? They hefted their wooden lances and checked their leather shields. The gold ornaments they wore glittered in the sun.

The battle began. The Spaniards fired their guns, and the Indians were shocked to see some of their men fall. Who were these men, that they could kill without touching their foe?

The Spaniards unleashed their dogs. The vicious animals ripped and tore at the Indians. The Spaniards cut, stabbed, and hacked with their metal weapons. The Indians' wooden arrows and lances, hardened in fire, bounced off the Spanish armor.

It was over quickly. Six hundred Quarecan warriors were dead. Not one Spaniard had been lost.

The next day, the leader of the Spaniards climbed a mountainside and looked to the south. What he saw brought him to his knees in excitement and gratitude. Blue water stretched as far as he could see. White waves curled onto the shore. An ocean! It was what he had worked and prayed and fought to find.

The man's name was Vasco Núñez de Balboa. The date was September 25, 1513. The mountain was in the country we now call Panama. The ocean, which Balboa named the South Sea, was the one we know today as the Pacific. It lay to the south because of the way the Isthmus of Panama, the strip of land that joins North and South America, twists at that point.

Balboa was not the first to see the Pacific. He'd been told of it and led to it by the native people. But he was the first person from Europe, the Old World, to find and claim the vast ocean for his king.

Balboa motioned to his companions to join him. They clambered up and looked out over the water. Many of them fell to their knees, too. Balboa and the expedition's priest directed them to build an altar of stones, and they fashioned a cross from a tree. They carved the initials *F* and *J* on it to honor their king, Ferdinand, and his daughter Juana. A notary recorded each man's name. There were sixty-seven of them. Some others had been wounded in battle the day before and had stayed behind in Quareca to recover.

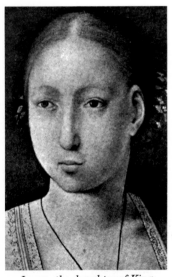

Juana, the daughter of King Ferdinand and Queen Isabella

Balboa sighting the Pacific Ocean

Balboa and his men admired the sea again before starting down the mountain. Now they faced yet another battle. Chiapes, a fierce Indian chief with a huge army, waited between them and the seashore. The Spaniards fought again, and the result was another victory. Balboa fought only until Chiapes surrendered. Then he pledged his friendship to the chief. Chiapes allowed the exhausted explorers to rest in his village for a few days, then provided men to guide Balboa and his men to the seashore.

At the beach, holding his sword high in one hand and a banner from Spain in the other, Balboa waded into the water until it covered his knees. Then he claimed the sea and all the lands it touched for the crown of Spain, "both now and in all time, as long as the world endures, and unto the final day of judgment of all mankind."

Chapter 2
Discovery of the New World

Historians aren't sure where Vasco Núñez de Balboa was born. Most accounts say that he was from the town of Jerez de los Caballeros in Spain, and that he was born in about 1475. His family, apparently, was neither important nor wealthy, though they were of the noble rank called *hidalgo*. Young men of such families were expected to gain glory through fighting in wars, and Balboa was sent at an early age to be a page at the court of Don Pedro Puertocarrero, the lord of Moguer.

The historian Peter Martyr wrote that Balboa was a master of the sword. Judging from his success among the rough and desperate men in the New World, Balboa must indeed have been skillful with his sword. Young men of the time and of Balboa's rank studied fencing and other arts of war as regularly as young people of our time study mathematics and reading. They worked and practiced for the day they would have the chance to fight for God and their king against the Moors, who occupied southern Spain.

Before 1479, Spain was divided into two kingdoms, Aragon and Castile. Then King John II of Aragon died, and his son Ferdinand inherited his crown. Ferdinand was married to Isabella, queen of Castile. The two monarchs joined their kingdoms and formed a united Spain. They were determined to have a completely Christian Spain, too. The Moorish invaders practiced the Muslim religion. The Christians believed it was their duty to force people of other faiths to convert to Christianity. The war against the Moors continued for years.

As Balboa was growing up, the world around him was changing. For centuries, Spain and the rest of Europe had avoided sailing on the Atlantic Ocean out of sight of land. Ships weren't built to withstand the roughness of the open sea, and instruments for navigating weren't very precise. Europeans needed spices and herbs from Asian lands such as China and Indonesia, lands known then as the Indies, the Orient, or simply the East. They obtained these goods by sailing east on the Mediterranean and then making overland journeys to trade for the precious items.

It may seem crazy now that people would work so hard and even risk their lives to get pepper and other spices we can easily buy for ourselves at any grocery store. But before there were refrigerators, meat quickly spoiled. People used spices to preserve their food and to cover the taste of rotting meat. Herbs from the East were also used as medicines. Wealthy Europeans also paid high prices for dyes, fine cloth, and exotic wood found only in the Orient.

In 1453 the Turks had conquered Constantinople, a city located at the entrance to the Black Sea from the Mediterranean. This city had been vital to the

A fifteenth-century sailing ship

trade routes between Europe and the East. The Turks made it increasingly expensive to do trade through Constantinople. European merchants responded by looking for other routes and markets. They began to carry heavier cargoes, such as grain, wine, and timber. Heavier cargoes called for heavier ships. Heavier ships could weather the Atlantic Ocean more safely.

The design of the ships changed, too. Sails were improved so that ships could make progress even against the wind. Oarsmen were no longer necessary. And instruments for navigation improved so much that seamen could find their position even under cloudy skies. They no longer needed to remain within sight of land. The open sea was no longer such a terrifying place. Europeans began to wonder if they could sail west to reach and Orient and its riches.

Christopher Columbus unfolds his plans before Ferdinand and Isabella

Christopher Columbus believed that it was possible. He studied maps and charts and spoke with other sailors and sea captains. He tried to get funding from the Portuguese king for a westward voyage to the Indies but was turned down. Then he approached Ferdinand and Isabella of Spain with his idea. They appointed a commission to study his idea.

The men of the commission determined that Columbus's idea was absurd. It wasn't that they believed the world to be flat. It was that they calculated the distance from the Canary Islands, Columbus's last port before being completely at sea, to the coast of China. Their estimate of the distance was about ten thousand nautical miles (over eighteen thousand kilometers). To cover such a distance would require fourteen weeks at sea. No ship could carry supplies to last that long for its crew.

The men of the commission were right. Their estimate of the distance was close to what we know today—it is about 11,766 miles (18,935 kilometers) from the Canaries to Hangchow, China. Columbus, who believed it was half that far, was wrong. At the same time, he was right in a strange way. Between Spain and the Orient lay a continent. No one in Europe knew it existed.

Ferdinand and Isabella were interested in the idea of reaching the East by sailing west, but they were too busy with their war against the Moors to spend more time on it. They took the advice of the commission and refused to back Columbus with ships and money for supplies. However, they said, once the Moors were conquered, they might consider it again.

The war had been going on for years. Columbus must not have felt encouraged. But in 1492 the Spanish Crusade succeeded in subduing Granada, the last stronghold of the Moors. Those Muslims who would not convert to Christianity were killed or driven out of Spain. The war was over.

Ferdinand and Isabella turned their attention to Columbus again. They decided to fund his expedition. On October 12, 1492, Columbus set foot on a Caribbean island he believed to be part of the Indies. He didn't know it, but he had reached the New World.

Vasco Núñez de Balboa was about seventeen years old in 1492. He must have been glad about Spain's victory over the Moors—it would have been disloyal for him to be otherwise. But he must have been disappointed, too. He had trained all his life to fight in the war. Now Spain was at peace. What could a strong young man, whose greatest skill was swordsmanship, do to win glory for himself, God, and his country?

A knight in full armor

When Columbus returned from what he believed to be his successful journey to the Indies, the news electrified Europe. It was possible, then, to reach the Orient by sailing west. And there were new lands to be discovered, new people to be seen and conquered. Balboa and other young men like him must have thrilled at the news.

Ferdinand and Isabella rewarded Columbus by naming him *Adelantado*, Admiral of the Ocean Sea. He was to be viceroy and governor-general of all new lands he found. No ships could set out for the West Indies, as the new lands were called, without his permission. He was also granted a large percentage of any profits made by ships sailing to "his" lands. He continued to believe that the Caribbean islands he had found were the Indies. Though on his next voyages he explored the coast of what we now call Central America, nothing convinced him that it wasn't all simply a large island.

Columbus started a settlement on the island we now call Haiti. He called the island Hispaniola. The town was named Santo Domingo. However, he had no talent for running a town or a country. Ferdinand and Isabella, on the other hand, were very good at it. They understood that the New World could create terrible problems for Spain—or it could make the country wildly rich. It had to be explored and administered carefully and skillfully. Therefore, they didn't hesitate to break their contract with Columbus and install a new governor in his place. Columbus was brought home from the New World in chains.

Ferdinand and Isabella established an office that would be in charge of voyages to the New World. It was called the House of Indies, and Bishop Juan

Columbus watching for land

Rodríguez de Fonseca was appointed to head it. Bishop Fonseca was a crafty, efficient man who used his power to help his friends. He was empowered use money from the royal treasury to outfit expeditions to the New World. A wise man with the interests of the country at heart would have examined the records of the men who requested funds for voyages.

Bishop Fonseca may have examined records. But he wasn't looking for sailing experience or the ability to lead other men into dangerous and unknown situations. He chose men for how well they could flatter him, or how much influence they had with other powerful men. For him, it was the natural way to do things. It had worked in the past, and Spain was an old country.

Bishop Fonseca knew that if he chose men of the right personality, any glory they gained would also be his own. He didn't understand that the New World was just that—a new world. There were diseases and dangers there that no man could imagine. It would take men of courage, understanding, and practical ability to make their way in the New World. But the bishop sent one foolish flatterer after another to lead hundreds and thousands of men.

In truth, hundreds and thousands of men volunteered to go to the New World. Rumors flew about how gold could be picked up off the ground or fished from the streams in nets. Fruit, people said, simply fell from the trees to be eaten, and the natives were so simple and gentle that they could easily be frightened into slavery. All the young men who had hoped to fight in the Spanish Crusade were convinced that glory lay across the Atlantic Ocean in the New World. Vasco Núñez de Balboa was one of these.

Chapter 3
Balboa Reaches Darién

Balboa was about twenty-six years old before he had his chance to go to the New World. He signed on with Don Rodrigo de Bastidas, a wealthy Spanish notary. Bastidas outfitted two ships at his own expense and set out for the New World. His license, which he secured from Ferdinand and Isabella, entitled him to take gold, silver, copper, lead, tin, quicksilver, and any other metals he found, as well as jewels, pearls, and slaves. He could load his ship with monsters, if he found them, and snakes, fish, and birds. He was also allowed to bring spices and drugs back to Spain. One-fourth of his profit would go to Ferdinand and Isabella, and he could have the rest for himself.

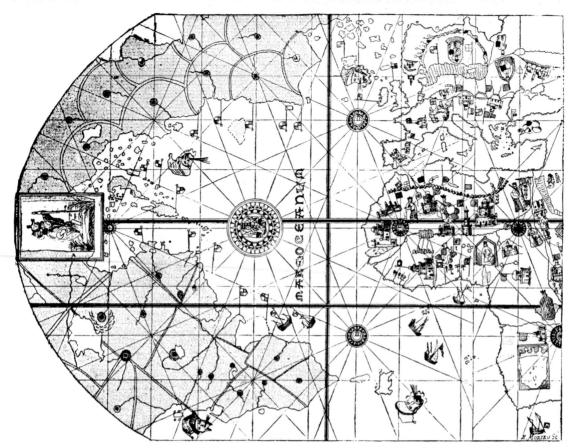

Map drawn in 1500 by Juan de la Cosa, Columbus's navigator. He drew west (the Americas, left) at the top and east (Europe and Africa, right) at the bottom.

To guide his ships, Bastidas hired the navigator who had sailed with Columbus. Juan de la Cosa had a great deal of experience in the New World. He and Bastidas decided to sail along the coast of what is now Venezuela. Taking a westward course, they traded for gold and pearls with the native people they met. Since the New World was thought to be the Indies, the Spaniards called these natives Indians.

Balboa must have paid close attention to the coastline and to the manners and customs of the natives. What he learned would help him greatly later in his life. He noticed that some of the tribes tipped their arrows with poison and some did not. And he noticed a pleasant Indian town on a river that flowed into the Gulf of Urabá.

Columbus coming ashore in Hispaniola

One of the biggest problems the explorers of the New World faced was a tiny sea worm called the broma. Broma worms eat wood, and they could make a ship's strongest, thickest timbers bend, leak, and snap. The two ships owned by Bastidas were soon too worm-eaten to continue the voyage. Juan de la Cosa turned away from the coast and made it as far as the island called Jamaica. There they took on fresh water, made some repairs, and set out for Spain. The ship was leaking so badly before long that they had to stop at another small island to do more repairs. When they set out again, they ran into a storm. Juan de la Cosa turned back to the small island until it was over. Finally they set off again, but they only made it as far as Hispaniola, where the ship sank offshore.

TRAMONTANA

ISOLA SPAGNVOLA

TORTVGA
ISABELLA VECCHIA
NATIVITA
P.S.NICOLO P.P.PLATA
C. CABRON
BAIOA
EPICH CIBAO CAIABO XAMANA
HV HA BO
GVANABA PANANA
S GIO LEVANTE
ONENTE CAIZCI M V C HIGVEY
GVACAYARIMA S DOMI NICO
C TIBVRON MONA
SAONA
S GIOVANNI
C. DE LOBOS
BEATA

Map of Hispaniola

The natives that Bastidas had captured to sell as slaves were in chains and therefore drowned when the ships went down. Most of the gold and pearls were saved. Bastidas divided his men into three groups and instructed each to march for the city of Santo Domingo.

The men and their treasure made it to the city, only to be thrown into jail. The governor of Hispaniola claimed that Bastidas had traded illegally with the Indians. Eventually Bastidas and his treasure were sent back to Spain, where the adventuresome notary was cleared of all charges against him. He was allowed to keep three-fourths of the treasure he'd collected, as his license had provided. There is no record that Balboa and the other men received anything more than their wages.

Balboa hadn't returned to Spain with Bastidas. He chose to stay in the New World. He was given some land on the southwest corner of Hispaniola, as well as some Indian slaves to work it. No one knows what happened in Balboa's life over the next seven years. Judging from the way he left the island and from things he said later, it seems that he was unable to profit from his farm and went deeply into debt.

It must have been boring and frustrating for an adventurer like Balboa to be farming—and unsuccessfully, at that—when there was a whole new world to be explored just a hundred miles or so to the west. His debts were like chains, because it was illegal for a man to leave Hispaniola without first paying everything he owed. In the end, it must have been too much for Balboa to take. He decided to leave the island illegally, as a stowaway.

Two men, Alonso de Ojeda and Rodrigo de Nicuesa, had been given a license to explore the lands east and west of the Gulf of Urabá. The man exploring the lands east of the gulf would be governor of those lands, and the man who explored the lands to the west of the gulf would govern that area.

Ojeda and Nicuesa were noblemen. They were young, and ambitious and charming. Ojeda had once shocked and delighted Queen Isabella by walking a twenty-foot (six-meter) plank that jutted out of the tower of the Cathedral of Seville. The tower was so high that the people below seemed small as ants. But Ojeda had walked swiftly to the end of the plank, kicked one foot into the void, then whirled about and walked easily back to the tower. Isabella had had to meet the brave young man, and he had remained a favorite at court.

Alonso de Ojeda walking a plank high above the streets of Seville

23

Nicuesa had served as carver to the king's uncle. His movements were deft and elegant. He was an excellent horseman, and he was often called upon to play his lute for members of the court.

The two men were charming, loyal to the king of Spain, and eager for glory. Nicuesa was rich. He'd been living on Hispaniola for a few years and had made a fortune capturing the natives and selling them as slaves. His fleet of ships carried more than seven hundred men with all their supplies.

Ojeda had already made an expedition to the New World. He'd sailed along the north coast of South America as far as the Gulf of Venezuela. His mission was to trade with the natives for gold and pearls, but he treated them so harshly that he got very little of either. Instead, he loaded his ships with captured Indians and returned to Spain, where he sold them into slavery.

When Ojeda arrived in Santo Domingo on Hispaniola, he was embarrassed to compare his puny number of ships and men to Nicuesa's. He asked Martín Fernández de Enciso, a wealthy lawyer, to become his partner. Then he could have more ships, men, and supplies. Enciso was to receive a share of the profits and would be mayor of Ojeda's settlement on the Gulf of Urabá. Nicuesa's ships left for the New World first. Ojeda's ships left a few weeks later, and Enciso's sailed two months after that.

One of the men Enciso hired to sail with him was Bartolome Hurtado. Hurtado was a friend of Balboa's. The two must have thought long and hard about how Balboa could come aboard Enciso's ship when it sailed. The plan they seem to have settled upon was, by most reports, to have Balboa carried aboard ship in a bar-

Ojeda on horseback

Balboa being carted aboard the ship in a barrell

rel. Then, when the coast was clear, Balboa apparently left his cramped quarters and rolled himself up in a sail.

Because it was so easy for men to arrive in Santo Domingo, run up debts, and then sail away without paying, the governor had imposed a strict rule. Each departing ship was followed by a police ship. Outside the harbor, before the ship left for the open sea, agents of the governor boarded the departing ship to search for stowaways. Balboa had to remain hidden until the police search was completed and the escort ship was out of sight.

Balboa exits the barrell

When he did emerge, the surprised crew called for Enciso. The lawyer was furious and threatened to have Balboa marooned on the first deserted island they came across. But the expedition members, some of whom were Balboa's friends, stood up for the stowaway. Enciso must have decided it would be worth having another able-bodied man who, the crewmen said, was handy with a sword. He allowed Balboa to join the expedition.

Balboa had left everything behind on Hispaniola—everything but his sword, his armor, and his faithful dog, Leoncico. He must have felt light, free, and eager as the ship plowed toward the west.

Alonso de Ojeda sailed to the mainland and promptly attacked the Indian village of Calamari. He and his raiding party took a number of Indians as slaves. Next, they ransacked the village for gold and any other treasure they could find. Then they marched inland, hoping to find another village where they could do the same.

They soon came across a town called Turbaco. It was larger than Calamari, and it was deserted. Ojeda authorized his men to loot the place. During the raid, the Indians returned and attacked. Every one of the Spaniards—except Ojeda and another man—was killed.

Ojeda and the other survivor made it back to the ships. They sailed west to the Gulf of Urabá, which was as far as Ojeda's license allowed him to go. If he had gone any farther, he would be trespassing on the land promised to Nicuesa. Ojeda and his remaining men built a settlement at the mouth of the gulf and named it San Sebastián.

The Spaniards didn't have much luck in San Sebastián, however. Every time they ventured into the jungle to find food, Indians ambushed them. These Indians put poison on their arrow tips, and men died quickly even from slight wounds. The Spaniards wore full suits of armor, but the natives quickly learned that any exposed flesh was fair game, and they aimed for the Spaniards' faces.

Because they were starving, the Spaniards were more prone to illness than ever. They were ravaged by tropical fevers. Every day more men died of sickness, hunger, or Indian attack. Finally Ojeda left a man named Francisco Pizarro in charge, took the best ship, and left for Hispaniola.

Pizarro waited for fifty days in San Sebastián. After that, he had authority from Ojeda to take the two remaining ships and sail east to Cartagena, on the coast of present-day Colombia. That was where Ojeda and Enciso had agreed to meet. When the fifty days were up, Pizarro took charge of one ship and a man named Valenzuela captained the other. On the way a storm came up, and Valenzuela's ship was overturned. All the men on it drowned. Pizarro continued on to Cartagena, where, with about thirty-five men, he met Enciso and his company.

It must have been a terrible sight, a terrible welcome to the New World. No doubt Enciso and his men had watched Pizarro and the others board their ships months ago, strong and hardy and eager for adventure. There had been between three and five hundred of them—reports vary. Now, less than forty men appeared like feeble skeletons on the beach, waiting for help and orders from Ojeda.

Enciso could not—would not—believe Pizarro's story. Even the letter Ojeda had left with Pizarro, a letter notarized in the Spanish custom, made Enciso suspicious.

He ordered Ojeda's men to sail with him back to San Sebastián. He claimed that they had stolen the ships and left Ojeda and the other men behind. Pizarro and the other starving, beaten men begged Enciso not to make them return. They offered him the gold they had collected, anything to be allowed to rejoin Ojeda in Hispaniola or even to join Nicuesa's party. Enciso eventually believed them, but he insisted that they return to San Sebastián anyway. His contract required that he start a settlement there. Otherwise he might not get to be mayor there.

A ship wrecked at sea

On the way back to San Sebastián, one of Enciso's ships hit a shoal and sank. The men were saved, but all the provisions, horses, and pigs were lost. And there would be no way, when the time came, to transport all the men in the party back to Santo Domingo.

They found San Sebastián burned to the ground. Worse, the Indians attacked more bravely than ever, and men died from the poisoned arrows. As they became hungrier, the men died of fevers, too. Enciso didn't know what to do and asked each of his men for a recommendation. Almost all of them proposed that they leave that place; but without enough room on the ships, that wasn't a choice that would work. And where would they go? Finally it was Balboa's turn to speak.

Indians in the Caribbean region

"I remember that in past years, coming along this coast with Rodrigo de Bastidas to discover, we entered in this gulf and disembarked on the western shore, where we found a large river and on its opposite bank we saw a town seated amid abundant fertile fields, and inhabited by people who did not put the herb on their arrows."

By "herb," of course, Balboa meant poison, which the natives made from the juice of a poisonous plant.

The men were desperate to get away from San Sebastián, and the place Balboa described sounded like paradise. There were about 180 men, and half of them took to the boats and followed Balboa's direction to the town, which was called Darién.

The chief of the town, Cemaco, assembled his warriors when he saw the Spaniards. He had about five hundred men under his command. Enciso's little

Indians washing the stream for gold

band waited until just before sunrise to attack. They were outnumbered, certainly, but their metal weapons and gunpowder made up for their small numbers. The Indians retreated and ran into the jungle, where they had sent their women and children before the battle. The Spaniards chased them for a while, but soon returned to Darién. There was food there, as Balboa had said there would be. And there was gold! The Spaniards rested, ate, and feasted their eyes on the shiny metal. Then some of them sailed back to San Sebastián and gathered up the rest of the party. Once everyone was settled in Cemaco's town, they named it Santa María la Antigua del Darién. Then they must have celebrated. They had not only avoided death in the New World, but they had found what it denied so many others—food, shelter, slaves, gold, and a sense of security.

Central American Indians sharing a communal meal, from descriptions by early navigators

The town was surrounded by fields, as Balboa had claimed. The men didn't recognize many of the crops being grown. Potatoes? They looked like big mushrooms—or maybe turnips. The men found that they tasted best when cooked. Captured Indians told the men that another crop was called *maiz*. We know it today as corn. The kind of corn that the Darién Indians grew had white kernels until it ripened, when they turned black. But the flour ground from these black kernels was white!

Another amazing plant was the cassava. The Indians used its root. The Spaniards were startled to find that the juice that came from the root was a deadly poison. But the Indians showed them how to wash it away. Then the cassava root could be used to make a tasty sort of bread. The Spaniards' favorite food dis-

Caribbean Indian dance, drawn from descriptions by early navigators and by historian Peter Martyr

covery however, was the pineapple. They all agreed that there was no other fruit on earth to match it.

And so the men of Spain learned to eat like the men and women of the New World. They might have laughed at the idea of it back in Spain, or even in Santo Domingo. But now they had been hungry, had seen their friends die of hunger. They were beginning to see that, though the Indians seemed to be primitive, they knew how to survive in the New World.

As the Spaniards settled into their new homes, the natives they had displaced returned from the jungle to trade for the valuable articles they had left behind. They needed their cotton hammocks and blankets and their cooking utensils. They didn't need their gold and were willing to give it to the Spaniards in exchange for their truly useful belongings.

Enciso, now that he was well fed and safe, was back in charge. He had lost most of his investment when the ship sank. But now he saw that the gold he and his men were collecting would more than make up for the loss. He became busy and self-important, making laws and issuing statements that made little sense to the men.

He soon made a law that turned the men completely against him. He declared that no one but he, Enciso, could trade with the Indians for gold. Any man found trading for gold and then keeping it for himself would be put to death.

This law showed the men how little Enciso understood or cared for them. They had left their families and possessions behind in Spain. They had faced the unknown, watched their friends die, starved, fought, become sick with tropical fevers, and faced death again and again. Had they done this to make Enciso rich? No! They must have muttered about it among themselves, then met in larger and larger groups. They had come to the New World to find gold. Now their chance to get it was being taken from them. They would not endure it.

Enciso had been a lawyer back in Spain. He often used his knowledge of the law to confuse and silence the men in his command. Now the men decided to use the law again Enciso.

The contracts issued to Ojeda and Nicuesa stated that Nicuesa was to have the lands west of a boundary line through the Gulf of Urabá, and Ojeda was to have the lands to the east of that line. Each had the rights to all the gold collected within his territory for the next ten years—minus, of course, a share for the king of Spain.

The village of Santa María la Antigua del Darién lay to the west of the boundary line. Ojeda had no right to cross that line, and once across it, he had no authority over his men. Enciso was in charge only because Ojeda wasn't there. Furthermore, the men must have reasoned with increasing hope, if Ojeda would have no authority over them even if he were there, then certainly Enciso had no authority over them either.

Under Spanish law, a party of men without a leader could gather and elect leaders by popular vote. The Spaniards in Darién decided to do just that. They met and declared that they would no longer regard the lawyer Martín Fernández de Enciso as their leader. They would no longer obey his laws. Then they elected a town council and chose two men to be their leaders. Vasco Núñez de Balboa was one of them, and Martín de Zamudio was the other.

Some people claim that Balboa must have stirred up the men so that they would get rid of Enciso and elect him as their leader. No one knows for sure what really happened. But to many historians, it doesn't seem likely that Balboa would have taken the time to do such a thing. His greatest personal interests, apparently, were hunting and exploring. It is more likely that the men looked to Balboa as leader because he had led them to Darién when they were on the brink of disaster.

The men understood that their government was only a temporary one. If and when Nicuesa arrived, they were prepared to accept him as their leader. Or, if Nicuesa did not arrive, they would write a letter to the king explaining their situation. Then they would abide by his decision.

Chapter 4
Darién Takes a Stand

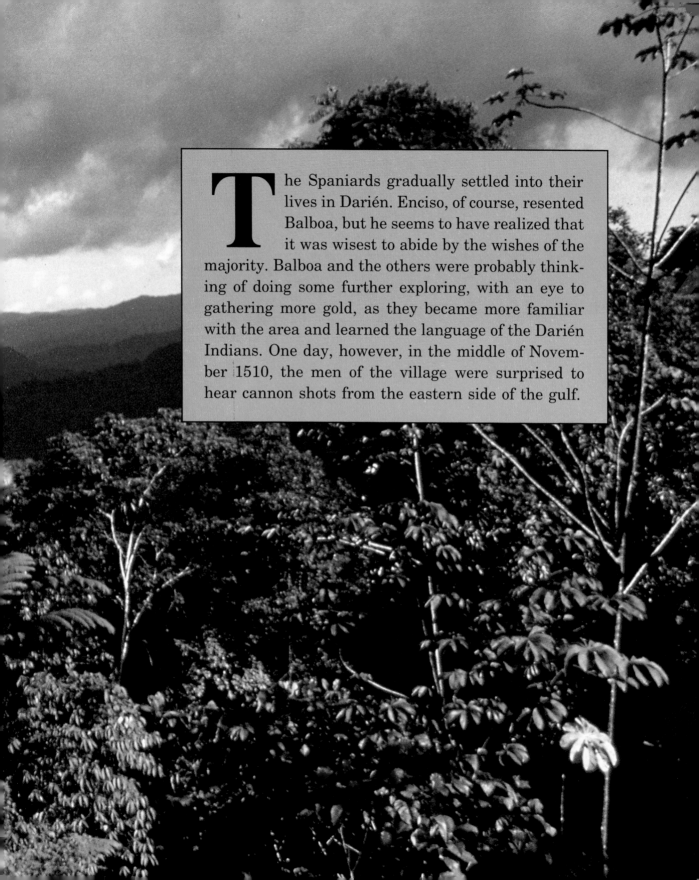

The Spaniards gradually settled into their lives in Darién. Enciso, of course, resented Balboa, but he seems to have realized that it was wisest to abide by the wishes of the majority. Balboa and the others were probably thinking of doing some further exploring, with an eye to gathering more gold, as they became more familiar with the area and learned the language of the Darién Indians. One day, however, in the middle of November 1510, the men of the village were surprised to hear cannon shots from the eastern side of the gulf.

They fired some of their big guns and sent up smoke signals, and within a few hours two ships anchored offshore. They were commanded by Rodrigo Enriquez de Colmenares, a friend and lieutenant of Nicuesa's. He'd stayed behind on Hispaniola to gather supplies and more men. He and Nicuesa had agreed to meet along the coast of Nicuesa's territory at about this time. Colmenares had already seen San Sebastián—what remained of it. He was glad to see a thriving settlement of Spaniards—but these were Ojeda's men. They had no right to be in Nicuesa's territory. Colmenares would have been within his rights if he had taken over the leadership of the town. He had more of a claim, under the Spanish law, than Enciso or Balboa.

Maybe Colmenares sensed that the settlers would not turn over power peacefully to anyone who came along in Nicuesa's name. Maybe he had no wish to lead a settlement. At any rate, there is no record that Colmenares tried to take over leadership of Darién. Instead, he seems to have offered them supplies and listened sympathetically to their story. The men of Darién grew to respect Colmenares, and when he sailed on to continue his search for his friend Nicuesa, the town leaders sent a committee of two men with him. Their names were Corral and Albitez. Their job was to explain to Nicuesa the reason they were trespassing on his land and to invite him to Santa María la Antigua del Darién to govern them.

Balboa, as one of the top leaders of the settlement, must have had a hand in organizing the committee. Maybe he even suggested it. There is no evidence that he was against inviting the rightful governor to Darién. There are reports, however, that Enciso and his friends were against the idea. Maybe they had something to do with choosing the men who went, for the two who accompanied Colmenares were enemies of Balboa.

Colmenares sailed west, searching for Nicuesa. After hearing the sad story the men of Darién had to tell, he was worried about his friend and leader. If Colmenares had had an idea of half the trouble Nicuesa had faced, he might have doubted that he would find him alive.

Nicuesa had sailed from Santo Domingo with seven ships and seven hundred eighty-five men. They'd headed for the Gulf of Urabá to get their bearings, then turned west toward the Veragua River. They were only the second to explore this coast; Columbus had sailed there on one of his voyages to the New World.

Columbus had found this coast to be rough and dangerous sailing. Nicuesa and his captains didn't have the skill for it—there were reefs and shoals, and the winds were fierce. There were no natural shelters for the ships.

During one stormy night Nicuesa's ship became separated from the others. He continued alone, and when he saw a river that seemed large enough for his ship to enter, he ordered his pilot to sail into it. He didn't know that the river was really a small stream— the rain had swollen it until it looked large enough to allow a ship to navigate.

Soon after Nicuesa's ship entered it, the rainwater ran off, the river became a stream again, and Nicuesa's ship foundered in the mud. The men had to save themselves. They watched from shore as ocean waves pounded their ship, and their food, weapons, and clothing washed away.

Nicuesa and his men had only a dinghy left, and they used it to continue along the coast, always to the west. One night, when they were camped on a small island, the dinghy and four sailors disappeared. Now Nicuesa and the rest of the men were marooned on the island.

They'd all but given up hope, when one day they saw a sail in the distance, headed straight for their island. On board were the sailors who had taken the dinghy. They'd been convinced that Nicuesa was wrong to continue sailing west. They took the small boat, sailed east, and found the rest of Nicuesa's party. Now they'd come back to rescue Nicuesa and the other men.

Something in Nicuesa must have snapped by this time. He'd come too close to death, perhaps. Or maybe he couldn't believe he'd failed so miserably. At any rate, he chose to blame Lope de Olano, his chief lieutenant, for the disasters that had befallen them. Once he'd rejoined the rest of the expedition, Nicuesa accused Olano of treason and had him put in chains. He would have had him beheaded if the other men had not begged in Olano's behalf.

By now all the ships were without food, and the men were dying of hunger and tropical diseases. They sailed east, trying to find a place to land, but the coast was inhabited by Indians who were not friendly to the Spaniards. Finally they saw a good harbor, one that had been used by Columbus. Nicuesa exclaimed, *"Paremos aqui en el nombre de Dios!"* which means, "Let us stop here in the name of God!" The men quickly named the place Nombre de Dios. They hoped it would be a lucky place for them, but they were wrong.

Nicuesa ordered the men to build a small fort.

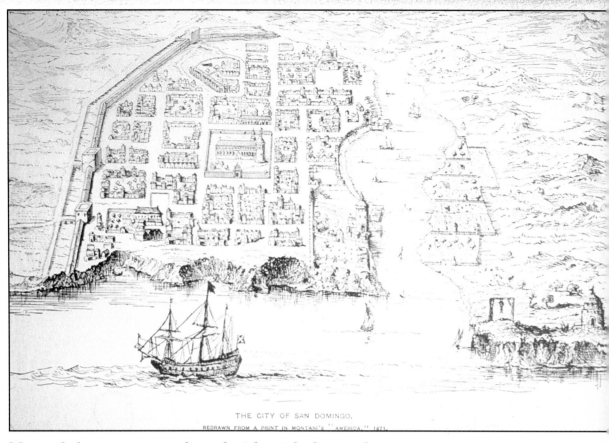

THE CITY OF SAN DOMINGO.
REDRAWN FROM A PRINT IN MONTANI'S "AMERICA." 1871.

Santo Domingo

Most of them were weak and sick with fevers, but Nicuesa refused to hear complaints. To men who were too ill to work, he said, "Begone to the dying place!" Of the 785 men who had boarded his ships in Santo Domingo, only a few were left.

Finally Colmenares, who had been sailing west to find Nicuesa, arrived in Nombre de Dios. One report says that he found two hundred men there with Nicuesa. Another report states that one hundred men remained, and still another claims that only sixty were left. Whatever the true numbers are, there can be no doubt that Colmenares found many fewer men than he had seen leaving Santo Domingo. And many of them were on the brink of death. Nicuesa and Colmenares embraced joyfully, and Colmenares was quick to pass out supplies to the starving men.

The two men sent from Darién must have felt glad, at first, to tell Nicuesa about their village. Nicuesa was so pleased to hear about Santa María la Antigua del Darién that he ordered a feast to be given for the two men from Darién. At the feast, after he'd eaten and drunk and was feeling happy and relaxed, Nicuesa told of his plans for Darién. He intended to take over and to punish all the men for having taken gold from his subjects, the Indians.

At first, the two men from Darién had tried to convince Nicuesa to make them town officials when he took over power in Darién. But after hearing about Nicuesa's intentions, they weren't sure they wanted anything to do with the man. Then they found Lope de Olano, Nicuesa's former chief lieutenant, in ankle chains. He said, "I sent relief to Nicuesa and rescued him from death on a desert island. Behold my recompense. Such is the gratitude the people of Darién may expect at his hands!"

Corral and Albitez told Nicuesa that they would go back to Darién to prepare a proper welcome for him. The sickest members of Nicuesa's expedition went back with them on the ship. In Darién, the two men told their story at a town meeting. The other citizens of the town were angry and alarmed. They had not come so far, worked so hard, or suffered so much to be punished by a man who would take what they had earned and call it his own. They turned to Balboa, who was said to have declared, "You are cast down in heart, and so you might well be, were the evil beyond all cure. But do not despair; there is an effectual relief, and you hold it in your hands. If calling Nicuesa to Darién was an error, is not receiving him a greater one?"

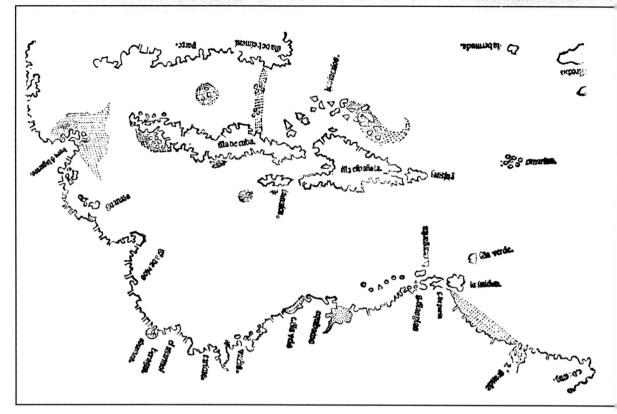

Map drawn in 1511 of the Caribbean region, including Hispaniola and parts of the Central American and Venezuelan coasts

It seemed a simple solution to their problem. The settlers decided not to allow Nicuesa to land in Darién.

Law and order was important to these men in the wilderness. What they proposed to do was against the law. They were, in fact, taking the law into their own hands. Most of the settlers had been trained as soldiers—they respected command. In the wild New World, even though Spain was thousands of miles away, they were to abide by Spanish law.

The settlers understood how serious their decision was, and they performed a ceremony in the little church they had built. Each man knelt on a cushion placed before a cross and swore not to receive Nicuesa as his ruler. Every man in Darién made the oath, and a notary recorded each man's name as he crossed himself and left the church. Enciso's name was on the list, too.

Nicuesa, of course, had no idea that the men of Darién would be anything but happy to see him. He sent ahead Juan de Quicedo, one of his men, to announce that Nicuesa would be arriving soon. Surprisingly, Quicedo was glad to hear that the settlers refused to accept Nicuesa as their leader. He confirmed the report of Corral and Albitez, saying, "What folly is it for you, being your own masters and in such free condition, to send for a tyrant, the worst man in the world, to rule over you?"

Quicedo also brought a letter from the imprisoned Lope de Olano to Martín de Zamudio, who shared the duties of mayor with Balboa. Olano and Zamudio were relatives and friends. Olano wrote of his unfair treatment at the hands of Nicuesa and warned Zamudio of Nicuesa's plan to punish the men of Darién. Those men needed no further warning.

They posted lookouts to announce the arrival of Nicuesa's ship. What happened after that is not completely clear. There are differing reports of what happened, and in a few years Balboa's life would depend on how and why Nicuesa had been denied the leadership of Darién.

According to one report, the settlers met Nicuesa on the beach and allowed him to land. After he spent three weeks as Balboa's guest, the men voted on whether they wished to have Nicuesa as their leader. When the vote went against him, Nicuesa argued and fought with Martín de Zamudio. He was then put aboard a small ship with some food, seven of his companions, and seven sailors. Then the settlers forced the ship out to sea.

Centuries have passed, so no one can be sure what really happened. But it hardly seems likely that the men of Darién would have entertained Nicuesa as a guest for three weeks. Another report seems more believable.

According to this report, the lookouts warned the men that Nicuesa was on his way, and they gathered on the beach. Nicuesa must have looked out at the little town with its thatched-roof huts among the green fields and felt pleased. As far as he could tell, the men were gathered on the beach to welcome him. Surely, then, he must have been surprised to hear what the town crier had to say.

For the town crier—backed by Balboa, Zamudio, and the rest of the men—shouted to Nicuesa that he would not be allowed to land. He was to go back to Nombre de Dios without putting foot on shore.

Nicuesa, shocked to hear exactly the opposite of what he expected, argued with the crowd but was unsuccessful. He ordered his men to sail back out into the gulf to wait for morning, when he hoped the men of Darién would be more friendly.

Nicuesa was allowed to land the next day, but then the settlers attacked him. Apparently he was a fast runner, for he managed to escape them until Balboa persuaded the crowd to calm down.

By this time Nicuesa was pleading merely to be allowed to stay in Darién, not to rule over it. Balboa must have felt that this was a reasonable request. He argued with the men to allow Nicuesa to stay. They wouldn't hear of it. One man was especially loud and disorderly, demanding that Nicuesa be sent away. Balboa ordered that the man be given one hundred lashes with the whip. This man, Francisco Benitez, remained Balboa's enemy for life. Balboa then urged Nicuesa to return to his ship for his own protection.

Some reports say that Nicuesa sailed away then. Others say that three men, friends of Zamudio, came to the shore and called to Nicuesa that the settlers had changed their minds. They wanted Nicuesa to stay. Nicuesa eagerly came back to the beach, and Zamudio and his friends, who had hidden in thickets there, attacked him. They captured him and put him aboard the worst ship in the harbor, added a few supplies, and forced him to sail away. Seventeen of his men chose to accompany him. The rest were allowed to stay if they promised to accept the present government of Darién.

However it came about, the citizens of Darién saw Nicuesa and his seventeen men sail away on March 1, 1511. No one knows what happened to him after that. There were reports that Nicuesa had been killed by the natives of Cuba after his ship washed up on shore there. Some people said they had seen an inscription carved on a tree in a region called Belen on the coast of South America. It read: *"Aqui anduvo perdido el desdichado Diego de Nicuesa"* ("Here wandered lost the unfortunate Diego de Nicuesa"). Another story tells that Nicuesa was killed by natives when he went ashore for water and food at the bay of Cartagena.

Years later, Balboa would be put on trial for the murder of Nicuesa. No other man from Darién would suffer for taking part in Nicuesa's bad end. And yet there was the notary's list of names of the men who had sworn not to accept Nicuesa as their ruler. There was the record of Francisco Benitez's hundred lashes, the whipping he had received for insisting that Nicuesa be made to leave. Even Colmenares, who had been Nicuesa's lieutenant and friend, did not stand up for him or offer to go with him when he was forced

The bay of Cartagena

to sail away. In fact, only seventeen of Nicuesa's men remained loyal to him. It seems obvious that Nicuesa had been twisted by his bad experiences in the New World. He was no longer the respected leader he had been before beginning his voyage. His own men no longer wished to be associated with him, much less to serve him.

Chapter 5
Conquests for Gold

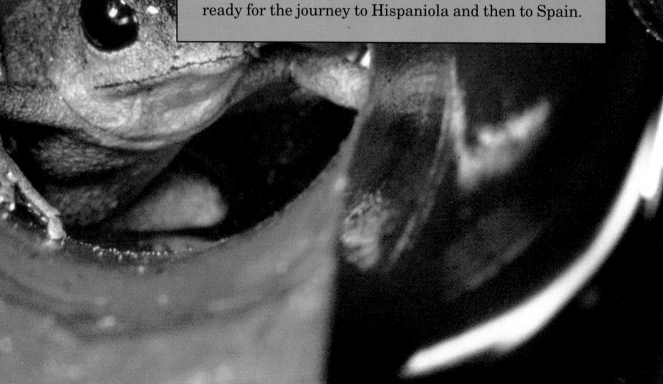
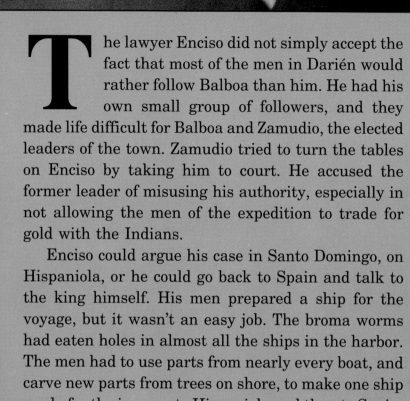

The lawyer Enciso did not simply accept the fact that most of the men in Darién would rather follow Balboa than him. He had his own small group of followers, and they made life difficult for Balboa and Zamudio, the elected leaders of the town. Zamudio tried to turn the tables on Enciso by taking him to court. He accused the former leader of misusing his authority, especially in not allowing the men of the expedition to trade for gold with the Indians.

Enciso could argue his case in Santo Domingo, on Hispaniola, or he could go back to Spain and talk to the king himself. His men prepared a ship for the voyage, but it wasn't an easy job. The broma worms had eaten holes in almost all the ships in the harbor. The men had to use parts from nearly every boat, and carve new parts from trees on shore, to make one ship ready for the journey to Hispaniola and then to Spain.

Ship sailing by moonlight

It wasn't very wise of Balboa to let Enciso go back to Spain. Maybe that's why he encouraged Zamudio to go, too. Balboa must have hoped Zamudio would remain loyal and speak the truth against the lies Enciso was sure to tell. But with Enciso and Zamudio on their way across the sea, Balboa was left in full charge. It must have been an exciting feeling for the man who had gotten to the New World by stowing away on a boat.

The first thing Balboa did when he had full command was to order Colmenares to sail back to Nombre de Dios. There he was to pick up the men of Nicuesa's party who had remained behind. As Colmenares was returning to Darién, his lookout spotted two or three Spaniards dressed as Indians on the shore.

Thick vegetation in Henry Pitier National Park, Venezuela

They were men who deserted Nicuesa's expedition the year before, when he'd been searching for the Veragua River. Indians in the area had found them and treated them kindly. This was the Indian province of Careta, and its chief was a man named Chima. The Spaniards whose lives he had saved weren't very loyal to him. They urged Colmenares to raid Chima's village. He had a good supply of gold, they said, as well as food.

Chima also had two thousand warriors under him. Colmenares wasn't prepared to take on such a force, so he and the deserters made a plan. One of them would return to Chima's village and the other one or two would sail with Colmenares back to Darién to tell Balboa about the Indians of Careta.

Balboa was interested to hear about Chima's gold and food. Some of the crops around Darién had failed and, with the arrival of the men from Nombre de Dios, the population of the town had grown. They needed food and, as always, the Spaniards were interested in getting their hands on more gold.

Balboa and his men went to Careta. Chima received them politely but claimed to have no food to spare and no gold on hand. Balboa was polite as well, and took his men away, as if they were returning to Darién. In the middle of the night they returned and attacked the village, killing many of the Indians and taking Chima, his family, and several of the Indians as prisoners. Balboa forced the captives to show him where they kept their food and then made them load it onto his ships. With the provisions and prisoners, he returned to Darién.

Chima seems to have been an intelligent and reasonable man. He saw that the white men were powerful, and he thought of a way to unite his people with them in a way that would work to their advantage. He said, according to reports, "What have I done to thee that thou shouldst treat me in this cruel manner? When thou camest to my village did I meet thee with a javelin in my hand? Set me and my people in liberty and we will remain thy friends, and cultivate the fields to supply thee with provisions. Dost thou doubt my faith? Take my daughter in pledge of friendship."

Balboa must have realized that he could have Chima's daughter no matter what her father said. Chima was his prisoner and Balboa was in charge. But he thought about the chief's offer, and he made a decision that was both wise and unusual for a Spaniard to make at that time.

A romantic drawing of Balboa meeting the Indian princess who was to become his wife

Most Spanish explorers regarded the Indians as pests, sources of food and gold, or slaves. Balboa seems to have respected and learned from the Indians. Perhaps he got this attitude from Chima, who remained his true friend for the rest of his life. At any rate, Balboa accepted Chima's offer. It would be better to have Chima and his people as friendly neighbors working to provide food for the settlers than to keep them as slaves and have to guard them. It was safer for a man to have friends than enemies. Balboa followed this policy with most of the Indian groups he met.

According to all reports, Chima's daughter was beautiful. There is no record of her name, but by all accounts Balboa treated her well and she was loyal.

Indians hunting with blow guns

Chima remained in Darién for a few days, eagerly watching and learning about the Spaniards and their ways. He was most impressed with their weapons, especially the arquebuses. He asked Balboa to help him raid the neighboring Ponca tribe. It would be to Balboa's advantage, Chima must certainly have pointed out. The Poncas had stores of food and gold.

Balboa promised to assist in the raid. He gave Chima gifts that delighted the chief—iron hatchets and knives from Spain. Then, reminding Chima that his people were to raise food for the Spaniards, he sent him and the other captives back to their village. But Chima's daughter remained in Darién with Balboa.

Balboa kept his promise to help Chima raid the Ponca village. He took eighty men to Chima's village. From there they went, with Chima's warriors, to Ponca territory. The Ponca Indians had heard of the white men, and when they saw that they had joined forces with their enemy Chima, they thought it would be better to run from the village than to fight. The invaders ransacked the village for its food and gold and then burned it. Then they returned to Chima's village. The chief was pleased with the way things were turning out. He asked Balboa to stay with him for a few days. The two men were becoming friends.

It was probably through Chima that Balboa learned of the great chief Comogre. Comogre lived farther inland and was ruler over ten thousand subjects. He commanded an army of three thousand men.

Through a relative of Chima's who lived in Comogre's village, the great chief learned of Balboa. He seems to have decided that it would be best not to fight the white chief. Instead, he sent an invitation to Balboa, asking him to meet with him in his town and make arrangements for peace between his people and the white invaders.

Balboa and his men must have been astonished when they saw Comogre's house. They reported that it was one hundred fifty steps long and eighty steps wide. It was built of stone and lined with beautiful wood. One part of the palace was a great hall, and hung from the roof of the hall were the bodies of Comogre's ancestors. They had been dried, wrapped in cotton blankets, and decorated with gold and pearls and precious stones. Comogre and his people worshiped the dead chiefs. It must have seemed weird and eerie to Balboa and his men.

Balboa amidst a quarrel over gold

Their attention soon turned to the gifts Comogre had for them. He had heard about how white men loved gold, and he presented Balboa with many beautiful, carefully worked pieces of gold jewelry, as well as seventy Indian slaves. The gold was promptly divided—one portion was set aside for the king, as always, and the rest was divided among the men. The soldiers began to argue over it.

Comogre had seven sons. The eldest was named Panquiaco, and he watched the Spaniards with interest and then disgust as they bickered. Finally he strode in among them and kicked the scales they were using to weigh the gold. Gold pieces flew, and the Spanish soldiers must have had their hands on their swords as the young man began to speak.

"Christians! What means this? Why quarrel over trifles? If you so love gold that to secure it you forsake your homes, and with so many fatigues and dangers come here to disturb the peaceful people of these lands, I will show you a province where you will be able to gratify your desire. But to do this, it is necessary that you be in greater number than you are now; for you will have to contend with great kings who will defend their lands with much courage and rigor. First you have to encounter King Tubanama, who has abundance of this gold that you value so highly, distant from our domain of about six suns."

River valley in Peru, the land Balboa heard was full of gold

Panquiaco went on to tell the astonished Spaniards about the great South Sea that lay over the mountains. Men sailed on this sea, he said, in ships, They used gold utensils for eating and drinking, they had so much of the metal.

Balboa and his men listened in awe as their interpreters told them what Panquiaco had said. Wasn't this what they had come to the New World for? They would discover this great ocean and find the people who used gold, it seemed, as the Spaniards used iron.

Panquiaco was the first to tell the Spaniards of the ocean and of Peru, to the south. He assured them that he was speaking the truth—if not, he said, they could hang him from the nearest tree.

Balboa and the men stayed with Comogre for a few days. Balboa talked endlessly with Comogre and Panquiaco. He wanted to know everything possible

Tiahuanacu, an ancient Inca city in Peru's Andes Mountains

about what lay between him and South Sea. Panquiaco believed that Balboa would need one thousand men to defeat Tubanama. He offered to act as Balboa's guide to the South Sea.

After Balboa returned to Darién, Colmenares decided to return to Spain. He promised to speak favorably of Balboa to King Ferdinand. Shortly afterwards, a ship arrived bringing two letters. One was from the king's representative in Hispaniola, appointing Balboa captain-general of Darién. The other was from Zamudio, who had returned to Spain with Enciso many months earlier. Zamudio was now in hiding. Enciso had told Bishop Fonseca that Balboa was keeping all the gold for himself and treating his men harshly. Fonseca believed his old friend Enciso and reported to the king. Balboa had been charged with treason. Fonseca was looking for someone to take Balboa's place as governor of Darién.

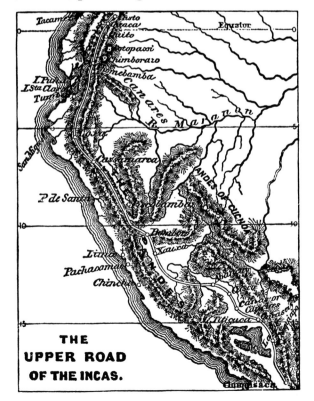

Map of a trail to Inca lands

Chapter 6
The Trek to the South Sea

Balboa must have felt sickened by the news from Zamudio. At the same time, he must have taken heart from the fact that Colmenares was on his way to Spain. Surely Colmenares would tell the king the truth about Vasco Núñez de Balboa. In the meantime, he would write to the king himself and explain his position. Then he would find the South Sea before a replacement governor could arrive—a governor who would snatch the glory from Balboa's hands.

Balboa had been trained as a solder, not as a writer. At least he could read and write—many soldiers at that time could not. But it must have been difficult for him to write such a long letter—eight thousand words! There was much to tell, though, and much depended on his telling it.

"Most Christian and Most Mighty Lord:" wrote Balboa, and he went on to describe what he had done to save and unite Ojeda's and Nicuesa's men. He told of his efforts to treat his men fairly, and he wrote that treating the Indians honestly "has been the cause that I have learned very great secrets from them and things whereby one can secure very great riches and large quantity of gold, with which Your Most Royal Highness will be very much served."

Then Balboa told the king about what gold he had learned was available. He hadn't had time or energy, he wrote, to hunt more for gold, and there were many times he had been more glad to find a basket of corn than a basket of gold. "We have more gold than health," he wrote simply. But with more men and supplies, Balboa informed the king, he could find much more gold. He described in detail the locations of various tribes who were known to have large amounts of gold. He explained how it could be gathered in large grains from the sides of the mountains. And he told the king of the great sea he hoped to find. He asked for one thousand men from Hispaniola—not from Spain. Men from Spain, he wrote, were not used to the New World and too many would die of the tropical diseases.

Balboa also asked for crossbows, as well as hand-guns made of a metal that would not rust. He also asked that they not weigh more than thirty pounds (fourteen kilograms) each! He would need ship builders, and mechanics to repair the crossbows, too.

He described several native tribes in detail and asked permission to capture and sell some of them as slaves. They were bad people, according to Balboa. By this he meant that they were fierce, warlike, and unfriendly to the Spaniards.

A Caribbean Indian mountaineer

Central American Indians preparing for a ceremonial dance

Balboa reminded the king that Ojeda and Nicuesa had together lost more than eight hundred men. He had made his successful stand in the New World with less than fifty men, the remnants of other expeditions. Now he had three hundred men under him, and he hoped the king would send him more, for he could discover great things. He described the gold he had sent the king before, which had been lost in a shipwreck, and the gold he was sending with his letter, and he signed himself, "The creature and Creation of your Highness, who kisses your most Royal hands and feet."

He sent the letter off with the ship when it sailed for Spain and he turned his attention to keeping his colony running smoothly. He would have to wait for the men and supplies he would need to discover the South Sea.

Forest in Costa Rica, Central America

Months passed, and they must have seemed endless for Balboa. No word arrived from Spain. In August of 1513 Balboa could wait no longer. He selected one hundred ninety of his toughest, most seasoned men and organized his expedition. The colony buzzed with the activity of outfitting the men. Eight hundred Indians, both slaves and free, were chosen to carry the Spaniards' supplies. Balboa chose lieutenants, organized weapons, and planned his route.

They left Darién on September 1, 1513, and took a ship and ten canoes to Careta's village. Careta was Balboa's father-in-law and friend. Balboa rested there for two days, talking to the Indians about the best route to take, collecting more supplies, and deciding which men should accompany him and which should

Forest dragon, a Peruvian reptile

stay behind to protect the boats. On the third morning he left his wife with her father, took his men and the Indian porters and guides, and headed into the jungle.

They worked their way across the swamps to the lowlands. Balboa had already written to the king about crossing the swamps: "Your Royal Highness should not believe that the swamps of this land are such light affairs that we move along through them joyfully, for many times it happens to us to go naked through swamps and water for one and two and three leagues, with the clothing collected and placed on the shield on the top of the head; and going out of some marshes we enter into others, and proceed in this manner two and three and ten days." Balboa didn't mention the poisonous snakes, crocodiles, or clouds of mosquitoes.

In the distance, they could see the mountain range that waited for them. It was horrid, heart-breaking work, this exploration. The men sweated and swore. But every one of them kept on, spurred by the drive for glory and gold. The Indians, of course, didn't have much chance at either of those.

After the swamps, the men entered the jungle and began to climb. They worked their way up the sides of the mountain until they reached the Ponca village that Balboa had encountered before. The Ponca Indians had hidden in the jungle when their scouts told them the Spaniards were coming, but Balboa coaxed them back. The leaders exchanged presents—Balboa gave the Ponca chief beaded necklaces, bells, mirrors, and the gift most highly prized by the Indians—hatchets. The Ponca chief gave Balboa impressive

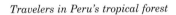

Travelers in Peru's tropical forest

amounts of gold, as well as offering him men from his tribe to act as guides and porters. Balboa sent Chima's men home with gifts and thanks.

Balboa had figured out the best way to explore the New World. He used Indian guides, who knew their territories as well as he knew the streets of his hometown. The jungle was so dense that the Spaniards quickly lost their sense of direction. The Indian guides, however, could find a path one footprint wide. Once Balboa and his men came to the end of their guides' territory, they found new guides. Then they rewarded the old ones and sent them home. Every conquistador after Balboa used this method. More than three hundred years later, Meriwether Lewis and William Clark used it when they explored the northwestern United States.

Lewis and Clark with Sacajawea, their Shoshone Indian guide

The Spaniards rested in the Ponca village, and Balboa discussed the journey ahead with the chief. He decided not to go out of his way to visit Comogre and Panquiaco, who had offered to guide him to the sea. It would take too much time and energy. The march ahead was long enough, and with the Poncas' advice, he felt that he would certainly find the sea.

He left the Ponca village on September 20. He and the men faced the real climb then—the mountains surged upward, and they scrambled up the steep sides, avoiding deep, swift streams, waterfalls, and the thick tangle of the jungle around them.

After four days they reached the mountain lands of the fierce Quarecans. It was because of the Quarecans that Panquiaco had said they would need a thousand warriors. Balboa had considered this, balancing Panquiaco's advice against what he had experienced in fighting the Indians on the coast.

The Spaniards carried steel swords, crossbows, and arquebuses—primitive guns. They had dogs trained to jump at the throats of the enemy. Balboa had seen that the Indians were terrified of dogs and the sound of gunfire. He knew that, as powerful as the Quarecans were, they would carry only animal-skin shields and wooden weapons. They could do the most damage with their sharp, fire-hardened lances, which they hurled from throwing sticks. A well-thrown lance could go straight through a naked man. But Balboa's men weren't naked. They wore steel helmets and armor.

Balboa also knew that the Quarecans had never been defeated. Still, this small band of fighters would look silly making a stand against the Spaniards. They had never heard a gunshot nor felt a steel blade. The warriors would be overconfident. And Balboa's men

Balboa fighting his way to Panama's coastal mountains

would be fighting angrily and fiercely—because they wanted to live and because they wanted to see this southern sea and gather the gold they'd been told they could find. Balboa believed that his men could defeat the Quarecans.

He was right. After the battle, after he and his men had collected the dead warriors' gold ornaments and searched the village for gold and food, Balboa rested with his men. He had defeated the Quarecans so thoroughly that those who were still alive treated him well, and he sent the Ponca guides back with their rewards. They left, anxious to spread the news of the Spaniards' unbelievable victory. Balboa chose new guides from among the men who had survived the slaughter. He arranged for the men in his group who were sick or wounded to remain in the village and be cared for by the Indians.

That night Balboa must have lain awake, wondering what was to come. He had crossed an ocean, the swamps, a jungle, and a mountain range. He had killed many men, and many had tried to kill him. He must have thought of Zamudio's letter and hoped he would find the South Sea and win the king's favor.

In the morning Balboa gathered his men, saw that the Indian porters had their burdens, and followed his guides into the jungle. A few hours later he climbed the peak indicated by one of the guides and saw the Pacific Ocean spread out below.

After their ceremonies honoring God and the king of Spain, Balboa and his men left the peak and started down through the jungle. They faced Chiapes, the warrior chief, and quickly defeated him. Balboa made peace with Chiapes before continuing on to the sea.

The Spaniards tasted the salty water, carved their initials in the trunks of trees, and enjoyed their triumph. The way to the sea had been hard on them. They'd climbed and slogged and fought their way across the isthmus, and it had taken them nearly a month to do it. Some had been wounded in the fighting, others were weakened by fever. They were glad when Balboa ordered them to march back to Chiapes's village. They would rest there, he said.

It would have been easiest simply to return to Darién by the same trail they had taken to the sea. Balboa, however, was considering a different plan. He found Chiapes was an intelligent man with an excellent knowledge of the surrounding area and the Indian tribes that lived there. Balboa spoke with him often, and the two men became friends. Balboa was quick to learn all that Chiapes had to teach him about the land and different tribes. He decided it would be

Vasco Núñez de Balboa

foolish to pass up the chance to see more of this country, its people, and—most of all—its treasure.

Chiapes told Balboa that the pearls in his possession had come from a neighboring tribe, whose chief was Cuquera. Balboa wanted more pearls—they were lighter to carry than gold, and nearly as valuable. Chiapes offered Balboa canoes and paddlers. Fifty Spaniards left with Balboa to conquer Cuquera, but they didn't have to fight. Cuquera and his people were so amazed and frightened by the Spaniards that they gave up immediately. Cuquera became Balboa's friend and gave him gold and pearls. He explained that his pearls came from oysters near some islands off the coast, and he pointed them out to Balboa. He would take Balboa out there himself, he said, but the autumn storms were so vicious that not even the best oarsmen would venture out at this time of year.

Balboa couldn't wait. He believed that God would watch over him and his men, because they were working to discover treasure in God's name, and Spain would use the treasure to fight enemies of the Christian faith.

Chiapes, Balboa, and sixty Spaniards set out for the islands in canoes. A storm blew up, and they were able to reach a small island. There they spent the night waist-deep in water, being beaten by wind and waves. In the morning the Indians patched their canoes well enough to get them to shore.

Now they had lost their food and other equipment. They had only their swords, and they were in the territory of a chief called Tumaco, who was ready, with his men, to fight them. The Spaniards fought for their lives, and Tumaco ran into the jungle with his people. Balboa coaxed him back with gifts, and Tumaco became another ally. He was a rich ally, too. Even his canoe paddles were studded with pearls. Balboa had his notary measure the paddles and count the pearls on them and record this in his notes.

Tumaco gave the Spaniards gold and baskets of pearls. The pearls weren't as shiny as the white men might have wished—the Indians valued oysters more for their meat than their pearls, so they cooked the oysters to get them open. The Spaniards were glad to show them how to open oysters without cooking them first.

Balboa and his men must have gotten dizzy just thinking about the wealth they had collected. But they couldn't forget what Panquiaco, Comogre's son, had said about the Indian tribe that used gold as the Spaniards used iron. Chiapes and Tumaco had heard of this nation, too. It was far away, but so rich that its

fame had spread up the coast and far inland. Tumaco called the nation Piru. We know it today as Peru. Chiapes and Tumaco were telling the truth about the people who lived there, too. The Incas had a great and powerful civilization high in the Andes Mountains. They were rich beyond belief in gold.

The ancient Inca city of Machu Picchu, high in the Peruvian Andes

Balboa couldn't look for the land of the Incas just yet. He had to get back to Darién and check on events there. He would need ships, as he had learned from his disastrous attempt to reach the Pearl Islands. He couldn't take canoes to Peru. It would be best to return to Darién, announce his discovery to King Ferdinand and the world, and arrange for the supplies and ships necessary to explore the coast.

His talks with Chiapes had convinced him to return by a different route than he'd taken to arrive. He and his men began the journey in canoes provided by Chiapes and Tumaco. They went up the river to the village of an inland chief named Teoca. Teoca had been warned that it was useless to try fighting the great white chief, and that the best way to make friends with him was to give him gold. Teoca was glad to do it. He offered men as guides and porters, as well. Indians from the villages of Chiapes and Tumaco would return to their homes with gifts from Balboa.

Indians mining gold in the mountains

The Spaniards' war dogs attacking an Indian chief

The Spaniards continued on their way through the jungle. They destroyed a chief named Pacra by throwing him to their dogs. Other chiefs in the area had accused Pacra of terrible deeds, and Balboa believed the stories were true. Also, Pacra insisted that he didn't have much gold, though Balboa's Indian friends (who were Pacra's enemies) said that he had rich gold mines. By killing Pacra, Balboa gained an even more fearsome reputation and made more alliances with native tribes throughout the region.

Nearly every chief agreed that Tubanama was the most powerful and fearsome leader in the isthmus. He was also the richest. He had heard of Balboa and bragged that he would drown the Spaniards when they came to fight him.

Balboa had fewer men than ever—those who had fallen ill were being cared for in various Indian villages they had passed. The men he had were tired and weakened by travel. He must have wondered how he could defeat this chief, who had a vast number of warriors.

Balboa marched seventy of his best men at their fastest pace to the village of Tubanama. They surprised the chief and captured him and his eighty wives. Balboa chose not to kill Tubanama, though he pretended to consider it seriously. Instead, he promised to release the chief if his people could pay him enough gold.

The Spaniards waited and watched, trying not to look impressed, as Tubanama's people filed from their homes carrying their gold and leaving it in a pile—a huge pile!—before Balboa.

Finally Balboa freed Tubanama, and the two pledged friendship. Balboa and his men explored the streams in the area and found the source of Tubanama's treasure. They easily found gold nuggets among the stones and gravel.

From Tubanama's village the Spaniards set out for the land of Comogre. At his town Balboa learned that Comogre had died, and Panquiaco was now chief. The young man was delighted to learn that Balboa had found the South Sea, and he took special pains to give the Spaniards plenty of food. They were thin and exhausted.

Next the Spaniards marched to where they had left their boats, the port village of Careta, where Balboa had left his wife and some of his men. From there, the explorers sailed back to Darién, triumphant. They had collected more treasure than any man there had ever seen all in one place before. They had discovered the South Sea. And they had not lost one man.

Balboa taking possession of the Pacific Ocean for the king of Spain

Chapter 7
Pedrarias Arrives

The men of Darién gazed in disbelief at the piles of gold, baskets of pearls, numbers of slaves, and all the cotton items Balboa and the others had brought back. Balboa set about dividing the treasure among his men. First, the proper portion was set aside for the king. To this Balboa added two hundred fine pearls. Then he divided the rest among the men, according to their participation in the adventure. Even the dogs were rewarded. The men who had stayed behind received slaves and cotton articles, such as hammocks. Balboa divided the booty so fairly that not one man complained.

Four ships had arrived from Hispaniola just before the explorers returned. They brought supplies and new recruits. They also brought a spy from the king.

King Ferdinand respected Bishop Fonseca, but he knew that the man could hold grudges and had been known to make decisions based on jealousy. The king decided to find out for himself how things went in Darién. Was Balboa a tyrant and a rough upstart? Would he try to prevent the landing of a governor to replace him? Ferdinand sent Pedro de Arbolancha to find out. Arbolancha pretended to be a trader. As he traded with the men he talked with them about their leader, Balboa.

Arbolancha learned that Balboa was fair, and that he did not put on airs. He worked, as all the men did, in his fields. His house was no bigger than anybody else's. Arbolancha had seen him divide the treasure from the expedition. After speaking with Balboa and watching him among the Indians and his men, Ferdinand's spy had no doubts. He would return to Spain singing Balboa's praises to the king.

Unfortunately, because of the broma worms, there were no ships fit to take Arbolancha back to Hispaniola when he finally decided to go. It would take two months to dismantle the ships they had and then make one seaworthy ship from the parts that were still good. Arbolancha must have thought with dismay of what Fonseca could accomplish in his absence. Balboa began to write a long report to the king.

Sitting down and writing wasn't something Balboa enjoyed, but it must have been wonderful to tell the king about the sea he had discovered, the treasure he had collected, the Indians he had met and conquered, all in the name of the king and Juana. When the ship was finished in April, Balboa bid a fond and hopeful farewell to his friend Arbolancha and entrusted his letter to his care.

There were now about five hundred Spanish inhabitants in Darién. Indian wives, slaves, and free workers brought the population to about fifteen hundred. The town was orderly, with sturdy houses and streets that were crooked but wide and clean. The fields were carefully maintained, and everyone had work to do. Life in Darién was good.

It was good until the end of June that year. Then a stranger arrived. He was beautifully dressed in silk and wool, with a plume on his hat. As he walked the streets of the town, he must have attracted a lot of wondering attention from the citizens. And he must have wondered, too, at how small and poor Darién seemed. He'd expected a golden city.

And surely he'd expected more of Balboa than this plain man dressed in cotton shirt and breeches, wearing rope sandals and helping to thatch the roof of a house. The two must have stared at one another. Perhaps Balboa could remember wearing such finery himself.

The young, beautifully dressed man was a messenger from the new governor, Pedrarias. He told Balboa that the governor had arrived and was anchored with twenty-two ships in the gulf.

It must have been a terrible shock and disappointment to Balboa, after all he'd done to make Darién a success. The news surely meant that the king had not yet heard from Arbolancha. Balboa must certainly have considered fighting for his town, but he didn't. He told the messenger to tell Pedrarias that he was "much pleased at his coming, that he would be welcomed, and that he and all the people of the town were loyal to the king and ready to receive the new governor."

Fashionable Spaniards dressed in the style of the day

The next day, June 30, 1514, the new governor came ashore with his wife, several officials and priests, and an army of fighting men. They formed a procession to walk into Darién. The new governor and his wife wore their finest clothes. There had been a ban on wearing silk and other finery in the New World, but for this governor and his expedition, the king had lifted it. The bishop, walking beside the governor, wore formal robes. Then came the officials and a group of bodyguards, wearing helmets and flashing armor. Next were priests, followed by hundreds of soldiers, craftsmen, and even women and children. Everyone was beautifully dressed in the latest Spanish fashions. They looked as if they were on parade in Seville.

In truth, these people had been on parade in Seville only three months before. This is their story.

The letter Balboa had written describing the possibility of a southern sea and the great wealth to be found there had arrived in Spain. King Ferdinand read it. He was excited that Spain should be in a position to win so great a prize. He acted quickly, authorizing Bishop Fonseca to put together a great expedition that would land in Darién and carry on to discover the South Sea. And, because of the reports that the king had heard from Enciso, he also decided to allow Fonseca to choose a new governor for Darién, someone to replace Balboa.

Even Spaniards who knew little of the New World protested that Pedrarias wasn't qualified to lead an important colony and expedition. But Fonseca insisted that Pedrarias was a man who had learned to flatter and impress powerful people. He enjoyed easy living and fancy clothing. He knew nothing of life on a frontier or of leading men responsibly.

The king approved Pedrarias and gave him the official power to fight and defeat Balboa, if necessary, to take over the governorship of Darién. He was also to discover the South Sea and to conquer natives and take their land and gold and the natives themselves as slaves when necessary.

Balboa had been counting on Colmenares to speak up for him to the king. But when Colmenares arrived in Spain, he saw that the powerful Bishop Fonseca had already convinced the king that a new governor was necessary. Colmenares didn't dare speak up for Balboa. He thought the king might not believe him, and then he would no longer be welcome at court. So he said nothing to change the king's mind.

Darién was an Indian name. Balboa and his men had named it Santa María la Antigua del Darién, but they were used to calling it Darién. In Spain, little Darién was given a new name, Castilla del Oro. That means "Golden Castile."

Balboa had told the king he would need a thousand men to fight the warlike mountain tribes he would meet on the way to the South Sea. Applications flooded Fonseca's House of Indies. Everyone wanted to go to Castilla del Oro. Balboa had written too glowingly of how easily gold was to be found there. Fonseca and Pedrarias decided to make two thousand positions available.

The men who came as soldiers had been trained to use their fighting skills against the French. They had bought themselves beautiful armor and expensive silk clothing to wear as they rode off to battle. But then King Ferdinand decided not to fight the French. The young, splendidly outfitted men fit the saying exactly—they were all dressed up with no place to go.

Fortunately, there was an exciting expedition to the New World in the works. Fonseca and Pedrarias were careful to choose young men of the most noble and powerful background. They didn't care too much about experience or skill.

Besides the soldiers, there were merchants, skilled tradesmen, and colonists, people who hoped to make a living from the land. And, of course, there were officials. A place with a name like Castilla del Oro needed a treasurer, an auditor, a judge, an inspector, and a doctor. Fonseca also sent a bishop and several assistants and monks, as well.

The soldiers needed the finest military equipment, and workmen loaded ammunition and weapons onto the ships. Two thousand people would have to eat, so they stored enough food to last the voyage plus another month. They also stored tools, cooking utensils, nails, and other important supplies.

Pedrarias spent months putting his expedition together. King Ferdinand sent him notes, wondering why things were taking so long. Finally, in April 1514, Pedrarias and his officials and all the rest paraded through the streets of Seville down to the docks.

The ships set sail on April 11. If Pedrarias had delayed for another two weeks—or if Arbolancha, the king's spy, had been able to leave Darién earlier—the king would have known that Enciso had lied about Balboa. Bishop Fonseca would not have been able to make Pedrarias governor of Darién. Things would have been very different.

In Darién, after all the men and women of the expedition had arrived on the beach, Pedrarias stepped forward. Balboa met him and knelt on the sand.

Pedrarias had been expecting a rough, rebellious bully. This open-faced, respectful Balboa must have been a terrible disappointment. Pedrarias had wanted to arrive in the New World with a flourish by defeating Balboa and retaking the settlement in the name of the king. What glory was there in simply accepting Balboa's respects? On top of everything else, Balboa offered Pedrarias and his wife the use of his house.

Pedrarias had also come to the New World expecting to find and claim the South Sea for Spain. He must have informed Balboa of this soon after arriving, and surely Balboa had a lot of satisfaction in telling Darién's new governor that the sea had already been found. The news, unfortunately, seems to have made Pedrarias furious.

For now, he ignored Balboa and led his officials and the other people of the expedition in a slow procession into Darién. The veterans of the settlement watched with bitterness and pity. They saw the fine clothes and white hands of the haughty young soldiers. Certainly they remembered friends who had died and were buried here in the New World—men who had died under Nicuesa and Ojeda. And there was no mistaking the amazement and disgust on the faces of the newcomers. These new people, the veterans thought, had no idea what it had taken to build Darién. And they certainly didn't know how close death sat on every side.

The newcomers marched into the town they knew as Castilla del Oro. They had imagined a golden city. This place was worse than the smallest, poorest village in Spain. To them, it stank of marsh gas. Mosquitoes buzzed around them. They were used to heat, but this was the humid, choking heat of a swamp. The men of the town wore no gold, in spite of all the reports of its wealth. They were thin and yellowish, clad in cotton trousers and shirts. Their sandals were made of rope. All of them had brown, rough hands from working.

To the men of Darién, who had faced death by starvation, disease, and poisoned arrows, their town was an oasis. It was order and safety in the teeming, dangerous wilderness of the New World. To the newcomers, it was poor, dirty, and ramshackle. The new name of their town passed among the men of Darién. Golden Castile! They laughed bitterly. These new people would find out for themselves.

That afternoon Pedrarias ordered a council meeting. He read the orders of the king. Balboa was mentioned in two of them. He was to be removed from office, by force if necessary. And he was, with all his council and officers, subject to what the Spanish called *residencia*. It meant that he could not leave his house for sixty days. In that time, his records would be examined and anyone with a complaint against him could bring it up, and the official would examine it.

Residencia was a familiar Spanish custom, so Balboa probably was not surprised by the order. He couldn't think of anything he had done to give any man cause to challenge him. After the meeting he went quietly to his house to wait for the time to pass.

Pedrarias visited Balboa that afternoon to discuss the problems he would face in governing the colony. He was very polite. He asked so many questions that Balboa offered to write a detailed report. Pedrarias exclaimed that it was a wonderful idea.

Because he had nothing else to do, Balboa finished the report in a couple of days. He wrote about the Indian tribes he had met. He'd made treaties of peace with at least twenty chiefs. He also wrote about the country he'd seen and the places he'd heard of. He drew careful maps of his path to the South Sea and of the lands he had seen. Every detail of his four years on the isthmus went into the report.

Pedrarias skimmed the report, exclaiming with approval. It was just what he had hoped to get from Balboa. Then he ordered that Balboa be put under arrest and brought to trial. The information he'd given Pedrarias was the most valuable thing Balboa had. If Balboa had kept it to himself, Pedrarias would have had to treat Balboa more fairly. Balboa, with his vast knowledge of the country and its natives, would have had the upper hand.

Balboa was charged with murdering Nicuesa by driving him away from Darién. Other charges were brought against him by one of Pedrarias's officials, the new mayor of Darién. This man was well known to Balboa—his name was Enciso. He was Balboa's old enemy from the early days in Darién. He'd gone back to Spain and was one of the major reasons King Ferdinand did not trust Balboa and had appointed Pedrarias to be governor.

Enciso charged Balboa with stealing his goods. Balboa had to stand trial for each of Enciso's charges, and the lawyer made a charge out of every separate thing he had owned in Darién, including a jar of dried fruit. The trials dragged on for months. It would have been best for Balboa had he been sent back to Spain in chains, as Columbus was years before. By then, news of his great discovery would have reached the king. Arbolancha would have spoken up for him. It would have been obvious he'd been the victim of lies and deceit. But persons close to Pedrarias, the bishop in particular, advised the governor to keep Balboa in the New World.

In the meantime, the newcomers to Darién were starving. They'd turned up their noses at the cornbread and other Indian food the veterans had learned to eat regularly. They'd eaten the supply of food on the ships as if they could simply order more from the shops when it was gone. Now they bartered their fine clothing for bread. As they grew weaker they became more susceptible to the tropical diseases and fevers. Seven hundred died in the first month. So many died that a huge grave was dug and left open. Each day's bodies were laid in it and covered with dirt. Gradually the hole filled in.

Pedrarias and the people who had arrived with him didn't believe that they should work in the fields. That was work for Indian slaves, they thought. Spaniards on horses terrified the Indians, forcing them to work. The Indians had to sleep in chains at night. Those who could escape did so, but many Indians died.

The Spaniards thought most work to be done with the hands was below them. The streets of Darién—once neat, if not straight or splendid—had become filthy and littered with garbage.

One day a letter arrived from King Ferdinand. He had received Balboa's letter and heard Arbolancha's report. He'd written quickly to let Pedrarias know that Balboa was in his good graces. The king planned to "favor and reward" him. Balboa's heart must have leapt when he heard the king's words.

Pedrarias, of course, was dismayed by the letter. He decided to defy the king by keeping Balboa in *residencia*. Balboa's trials with Enciso were over, but his trial for the murder of Nicuesa had been suspended. Pedrarias could bring him back to court at any time.

Balboa had to be patient and wait for the king's favor and reward. It must have been hard to be patient, however, when he learned that Captain Ayora had tortured and killed men in Chima's, his father-in-law's, tribe. Chima was Balboa's good friend. Balboa also learned that Captain Ayora had tortured men in the Ponca tribe by hanging them over fire until they were dead. He had ordered that women and children be killed. He had destroyed Panquiaco's village, and Panquiaco, who had been first to tell the Spaniards about the South Sea, was dead.

A Spanish conquistador

Balboa had treated the Indians so well that, after he returned from the South Sea, he could have taken the same trail back to the sea again and not encountered an unfriendly tribe. He had fought the Indians when he'd had to, but then he'd made peace. Now the treaties he'd made were being ignored. Indians who had given him goods and who had cared for his men until they were strong enough to rejoin the expedition were being killed, tortured, or taken as slaves.

In March 1515, more ships arrived from Spain. Pedrarias received a letter from King Ferdinand that, for a moment, must have confirmed his greatest fears. Then, reading on, he discovered a loophole.

Balboa was given the title *Adelantado*, or Admiral. Only one man before him had held such a rank, and that was Christopher Columbus. He was also named governor of the South Sea and the lands of Panama

Destruction of an Indian village

and Coiba. And then, at the end, the king wrote that Balboa must have the permission and cooperation of Pedrarias before undertaking anything.

Pedrarias continued to keep the explorer in Darién as he sent out expedition after expedition. The men who went out returned with gold and tales of torture and killing. One boastful Spaniard claimed to have left forty thousand dead on one of his marches.

The Indians, who for the most part had been so friendly to Balboa, were quick to fight back. Their weapons weren't as good as the Spaniards', but they had the advantage of surprise and of familiarity with the jungle. They knew what the Spaniards were after—gold. So they gave it to each one they caught. The unlucky white man was tied to stakes on the ground, face up. Then molten gold was poured down his throat until he died.

At the end of 1515, Balboa decided to take matters into his own hands. He had waited long enough. He sent a friend from the early days in Darién to Hispaniola to recruit men for his next venture. Seventy men and provisions for the trip arrived, and Balboa went to Pedrarias and told him he would be leaving. He would be taking some men from Darién, as well.

Pedrarias ordered him not to go, but Balboa was determined. He organized two hundred men and found supplies for them. Then he went to Chima's village. Balboa had started a small Spanish settlement near there on his way back from the South Sea. It was called Acla. There, Balboa informed his men that they were not going to the South Sea just to start a settlement. They would go to the South Sea and sail to the Pearl Islands and then to Peru, the golden land he'd heard so much about.

Balboa and his men cutting timbers to build ships

Chima could help him. The Indian chief said that one kind of tree growing near his village was so bitter that the broma worm wouldn't eat it. Broma worms had eaten and ruined many of the ships that visited the New World. Balboa knew how important it was to have ships that were resistant to the pest. Chima told him that the tree grew only in his territory. Balboa trusted his friend's knowledge of the jungle and sea. He began an immense project.

He decided that he and his men would cut down the trees Chima showed them. Then they would saw them into logs and then timbers. Then they would cut and hew and carve the timbers into the pieces necessary to build four ships. And then, Balboa told his men, they would carry the pieces through the swamps, into the jungle, and up and over the mountains, down to the sea.

The men must have thought their old leader had lost his mind. It was difficult enough to get to the South Sea without carrying several tons of wood. And what would they do once they got the ships' pieces to the coast?

They would put the ships together and sail to the golden coast of Peru, Balboa told them. They would find treasure beyond anything they had seen yet.

It seems strange, but these men, who would not work for wages back in Spain or even in Darién, set to work cutting and carving trees. The labor ahead of them was backbreaking—they must have kept themselves going with thoughts of the gold they would find. Balboa, his men, and hundreds of Indians spent the year 1516 and part of 1517 fashioning the wood into pieces for their ships.

Back in Spain, King Ferdinand died. His daughter was mentally ill and could not govern, and his grandson was too young to take charge. A temporary government was set up, and it was headed by a man named Cardinal Ximinez, who believed that Indians should be treated humanely.

Cardinal Ximinez began his investigation of how Indians were being treated in the New World by sending representatives to Hispaniola. They reported on the horrible suffering endured by the natives there. The cardinal ordered changes. Indians were given land and villages and allowed to return to their old way of life. Just as they began to harvest their first crops, a smallpox epidemic struck. Thousands of Indians, already weakened by their unhealthy lives as slaves, got sick and died.

Cardinal Ximinez

Pedrarias heard about the changes and knew that an investigation of his treatment of Indians would land him back in Spain—in prison. Reports of how Balboa had formed alliances and friendships with native people would certainly win the explorer favor. It made Pedrarias sick to think that Balboa might yet get the best of him.

One day in Acla, where Balboa and his men were working, Judge Espinosa and some of his starving followers dragged themselves out of the jungle. They were near death from exposure and hunger. Espinosa was the judge who had presided at Balboa's trials with Enciso. And he was the man who claimed to have left forty thousand Indians dead. Balboa must certainly have despised the way he treated the natives, but he gave Espinosa and his men food and ordered that they receive care.

The time came for the journey to the South Sea. They left in the spring of 1517. Balboa, two hundred Spaniards, fifty black slaves from Spain, and hundreds of Indians picked up their loads and walked into the jungle. They had formed the ships' pieces with hand-held tools, and now they carried the massive wood masts, planks, and timbers on their backs. They also carried the anchors, ropes, sails, and other fittings necessary for ships. They struggled for thirty miles (forty-eight kilometers) through dense jungle, over deep and swift rivers, and up steep cliffs. Once they got to the top of the mountains, they rested. The trip down was as bad as the one going up. They brought their burdens to the River Balsas and floated everything to the coast. There were so many rough or shallow spots in the river that the men still had to carry everything much of the time.

Once at the coast, the men discovered that broma worms had eaten into the wood, after all. Already, several pieces were useless. Chima had been wrong. They stood and stared at the damage for a while, and then Balboa directed them to use the enough of the uneaten pieces they'd brought from Acla to build two ships instead of four. They used these ships to sail to the Pearl Islands Balboa had tried to reach before. Then they built two more ships from trees that grew there on the coast and sailed south toward Peru.

River in the Central American jungle

Ship tossed by a whale

They had sailed a hundred miles (one hundred sixty-one kilometers), when suddenly the ocean churned and foamed. They had run into a huge school of whales. Enormous flukes slapped the water and bashed again the sides of the ships. All around them the men saw smooth gray backs crusted with barnacles. Their ships were brigantines, two-masted vessels much smaller than the galleons and caravels that had brought them from Spain. Some of the whales were longer than the ships, and they rolled, dived, and spouted. They rocked the ships and tipped them dangerously close to the water. Balboa gave the order to head for shore.

1689 map of the Isthmus of Panama

They returned to their base. Balboa saw that they would need larger ships. He wrote in his journal that, in spite of how difficult it would be, Spain could benefit from cutting a channel through the isthmus. (The idea remained alive for four hundred years, until the United States built the Panama Canal.)

Soon after their return, news arrived that a new governor had been appointed to replace Pedrarias. Cardinal Ximinez had learned how Pedrarias had treated the Indians around Darién. He had heard that Pedrarias refused to discipline any men who murdered natives. Ximinez wrote to announce that the new governor, Lope de Sosa, would arrive soon.

Balboa was puzzled by the news. He wondered if this new governor would be more or less difficult than Pedrarias. Now that the isthmus was between them, he and Pedrarias had been on good terms in their letters. Balboa spoke to his old friend Garabito, who had gone on missions for him before. Garabito was to cross the isthmus and go back to Darién and find out anything he could about the situation. Balboa did not know that he was choosing a man who, in recent months, had begun to hate him.

Perlas Archipelago, Panama

Garabito wanted Balboa's wife for himself. The Indian princess would have nothing to do with him. She loved Balboa. Balboa had told Garabito to leave his wife alone. Balboa wasn't a man to hold a grudge, and he thought the bad feelings were in the past. But as Garabito crossed the isthmus, he thought of a plan to get back at Balboa.

Rio Chagres from the Trans-Isthmus Highway, Panama

Indians mistreated by the Spaniards

Garabito went to Pedrarias and told him that Balboa had four ships ready to sail for Peru, where he would be free to do as he wished because Pedrarias had no authority there. Balboa had three hundred men, Garabito lied. He said nothing about the whales, or about Balboa's real plans. Actually, Balboa was going to forget about Peru for the time being. He planned instead to build a settlement in the region called Panama, where the land was very fertile. He hoped to gain the cooperation, first by force and then by friendship, of the Indian chiefs in the region. They would help him and the other Spaniards to dig gold mines and clear and plant fields and build ships.

Garabito went on with his lies. Once Balboa reached Peru, he pointed out, he would gather up the wealth

Balboa meeting with Pedrarias

of that fabulous nation and be rich as no man had been before him. His fame would live forever.

Pedrarias apparently became as angry as Garabito had hoped he would. The governor plotted to get Balboa back to his side of the isthmus. He didn't want to meet Balboa in Darién—or Golden Castile, as he called it. Balboa had too many loyal friends there. Pedrarias wrote a polite note inviting Balboa to meet him in Acla to discuss supplies for the ships. To be sure that the men of Acla would feel loyal to him, Pedrarias sent supplies of wine, flour, oil, vinegar, and bacon to the settlement and had them sold cheaply, even on credit. He made sure the men knew that he was behind this act of kindness. Then Pedrarias and his officials went to Acla to act.

Francisco Pizzaro

The messenger who brought the letter from Pedrarias to Balboa warned the explorer that he suspected danger. Balboa shrugged off the warning and left his men under one of his captains. He took only a few men with him. Before he crossed the mountains he was met by Francisco Pizarro and a group of soldiers. Pizarro was the man Ojeda had left in charge of his men at San Sebastián. He'd been with Balboa through the taking of Darién from the natives, the difficult early years of the settlement, the discovery of the South Sea, and everything since. Now he'd been sent by Pedrarias to arrest Balboa.

It is reported that Balboa asked in surprise, "What means this Francisco Pizarro? You are not accustomed to come out to receive me in this manner!" Pizarro, apparently, made no reply. If Balboa could have seen the future, he would have learned that it would be Pizarro who would find, high in the Andes Mountains, the ancient and advanced civilization of the Incas. Their skill in science, mathematics, and astronomy would mean nothing to him, and their artwork—beautifully beaten and carved—would be important to him only because it was made out of gold. He would murder and loot and become the richest and most famous conquistador of all, before being killed by his own men. The Inca civilization he would destroy would be lost forever, known only through its ruins.

Machu Picchu, known as the "lost city" of the Incas

Balboa could not see into the future, of course, or he would not have made the trip in the first place. He could see that he had done nothing wrong and so he thought he had nothing to fear. He went with Pizarro and the soldiers to Acla, where he was thrown into jail.

He was charged with treason and with the death of Nicuesa. His trial was held quickly, and Balboa

One of many artists' renditions of Balboa before the executioner

was not allowed to defend himself. He was found guilty and sentenced to death.

On a day between the tenth and twentieth of January 1519, Balboa was led from the jail into the town plaza. He wore chains on his arms and legs. He knelt, and a priest blessed him. Then he rose and went to the block. He rested his head on it. A blade flashed, and Vasco Núñez de Balboa was dead.

Another version of Balboa's execution

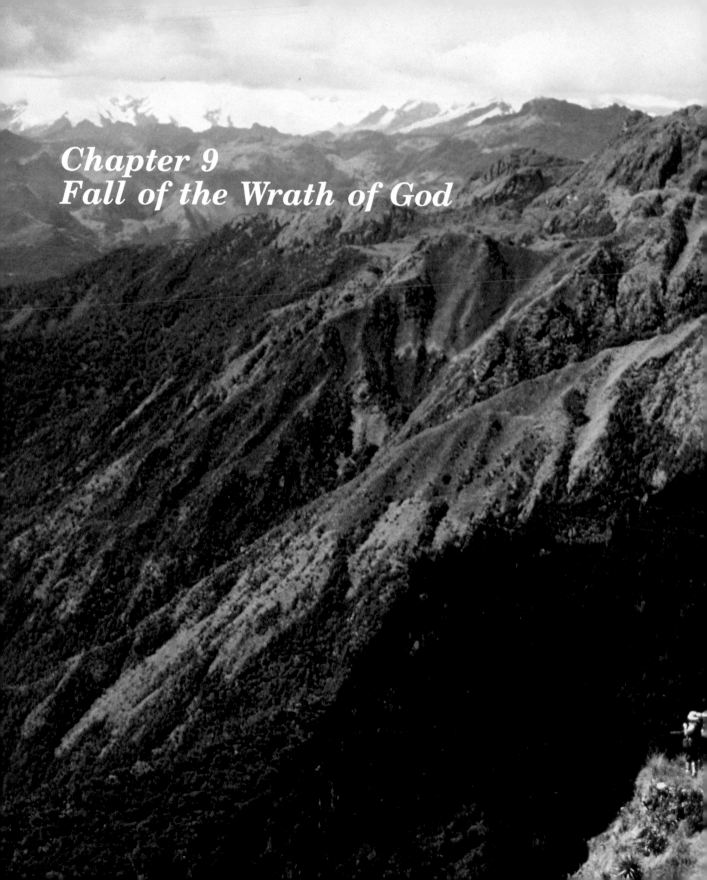

Chapter 9
Fall of the Wrath of God

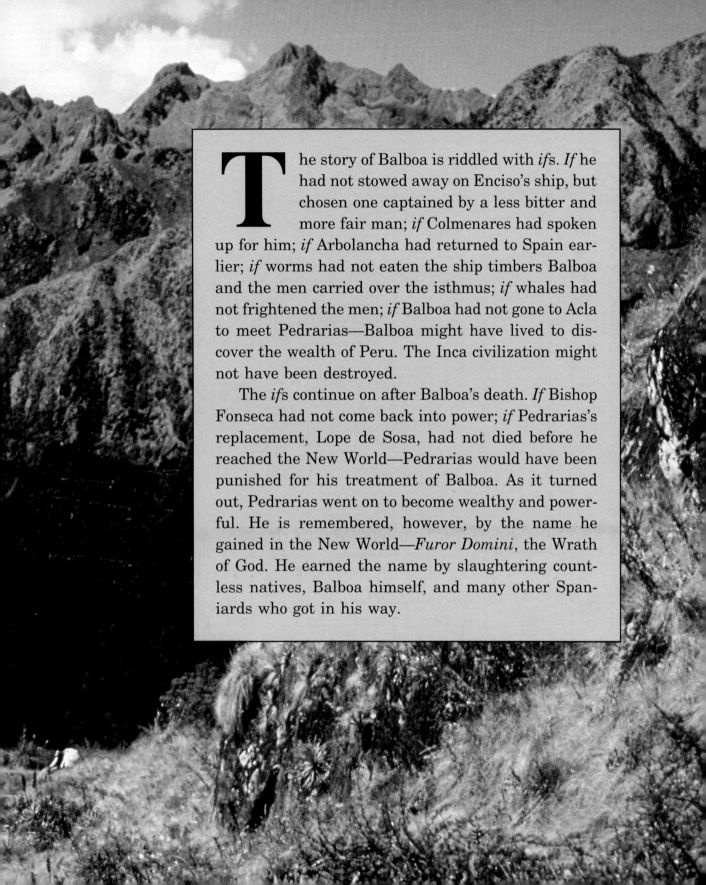

The story of Balboa is riddled with *if*s. *If* he had not stowed away on Enciso's ship, but chosen one captained by a less bitter and more fair man; *if* Colmenares had spoken up for him; *if* Arbolancha had returned to Spain earlier; *if* worms had not eaten the ship timbers Balboa and the men carried over the isthmus; *if* whales had not frightened the men; *if* Balboa had not gone to Acla to meet Pedrarias—Balboa might have lived to discover the wealth of Peru. The Inca civilization might not have been destroyed.

The *if*s continue on after Balboa's death. *If* Bishop Fonseca had not come back into power; *if* Pedrarias's replacement, Lope de Sosa, had not died before he reached the New World—Pedrarias would have been punished for his treatment of Balboa. As it turned out, Pedrarias went on to become wealthy and powerful. He is remembered, however, by the name he gained in the New World—*Furor Domini*, the Wrath of God. He earned the name by slaughtering countless natives, Balboa himself, and many other Spaniards who got in his way.

Soon after Balboa was killed, Pedrarias gathered an army and marched to the South Sea. There he proclaimed he had discovered it himself, and ordered the notaries and scribes to write it all down. When he got back to Darién, he ordered that Balboa's name be erased from all documents connecting him with the discovery of the South Sea. The men who had known and loved Balboa, however, did not forget the truth. For years it was a sign of a man's evil character if others called him, in secret, Pedrarias.

One story about Balboa has lived through the centuries. When it was time for Pedrarias to make his own *residencia*, as Balboa had, he posted a sign in the plaza in Acla. It ordered the settlers who wanted to make charges against him to come to his new headquarters on the shore of the sea he had discovered. Men read the sign and stood about, talking. A herd of horses grazed nearby. One of the mares had been Balboa's favorite. The horse left all the others and trotted over to the sign. She ripped the paper off the post with her teeth, trampled it into the ground, and returned to the herd.

In 1520, the sea Balboa had claimed for Spain was named the Pacific Ocean by Ferdinand Magellan, who was first to sail across it and around the world. The Panama Canal, which got its start with Balboa's journal entry, is flanked on the Pacific side by a city named Balboa. As people in the United States use dollars and people in Spain use pesos, the people of Panama use a unit of money called the balboa.

Like Francisco Pizarro and other conquistadors, Balboa was in the New World for gold. When Indians stood between him and his goal, he killed them. He was different from the other men, however, in that he

Ferdinand Magellan

believed in alliances rather than wars. He had Indian friends. He saw the Indians as people, not simply as part of the loot to be found in the New World. If he had lived, and if others had followed his example, maybe the historian Peter Martyr, who kept records of explorations, would not have written in a letter to the Pope:

> *I shall recount what happened in a few words, for the story is not pleasing; in fact it is quite the contrary. There has been nothing but killing and being killed, massacring and being massacred.*

Balboa overlooking the Pacific Ocean

Appendices

Part of a letter from Balboa to King Ferdinand:

Until now we have valued the eatables more than
the gold, for we have more gold than health, and
often I have searched in various directions, desir-
ing more to find a sack of corn than a bag of gold.
. . . The Indians go into the water and gather the
gold in baskets. They also scrape it up in the beds
of streams, when they are dry. . . . Those Indians
who eat men . . . have no workshops nor do they
support themselves on anything but fish, which
they exchange for maize.

Part of a letter from King Ferdinand to Balboa, which
the explorer received while he was on trial for
unjust charges:

This will be only to tell you how greatly I was
rejoiced to read your letters and to learn of the
things you discovered in those regions of Terra
Nueva de la Mar del Sur. . . . As regards yourself, I
will so dispose that you be honored and your serv-
ices recompensed. . . . I am pleased with the way
you behaved to the chiefs on that march, with kindness and forbearance. . . . When your letters came,
Pedrarias had already left. I am writing to him to
look to your affairs with care and to favor you as a
person whom I greatly desire to gratify and who
has greatly served me, and I am sure that he will
do so.

Opposite page: A fifteenth-century sailing ship

Part of a letter from Balboa to King Ferdinand about Pedrarias:

With regard to the governor, although he is a distinguished personage, your Highness knows that he is very old to serve in these parts, and he suffers greatly from a serious illness so that he has never been well for a single day since he came here. He is an excessively hasty man; he is a man who does not much care even if half the troops are lost on the expeditions. He has never punished the destruction and killings done in the entradas both to chiefs and Indians. . . . Pedrarias is a person who is delighted to see discord between people, and if there is none he creates it, speaking ill of one to the other; this vice he has to a very great extent. He is a man who, absorbed in his profit getting and greed, does not remember that he is Governor or occupy himself with anything else; because it matters nothing to him whether the whole world be lost or won. . . .

Part of a letter Pedrarias wrote to the Spanish court about Balboa:

What must be said about Vasco Núñez is his character, and how it is public and notorious that he does not know how to speak the truth. . . . that he has no love or good will for any worthy person, but likes to converse and be intimate with people of low degree. That he is most excessively avaricious; covets greatly any good thing possessed by another; is very cruel and disagreeable; never forgives; never submits to any advice; has no self-control nor can use any to resist any vicious appetite; is very mercenary; has neither obedience nor reverence for the Church and her ministers; is of most evil conscience; is always set on tricking the person with whom he converses. . . .

The island of Hispaniola and the northeast coast of South America appear on the left of this 1513 map.

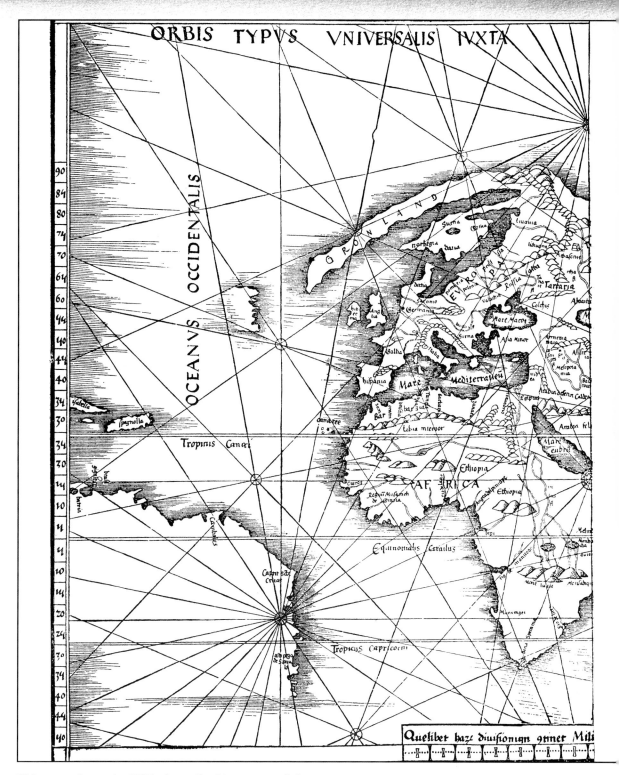

This map, drawn in 1527, shows Darién at center left.

Timeline of Events in Balboa's Lifetime

1475—Vasco Núñez de Balboa is born, probably in Jerez de los Caballeros, Spain

1479—King Ferdinand of Aragon marries Queen Isabella of Castile, joining their kingdoms in a united Spanish empire

1480—Ferdinand Magellan is born in Portugal; end of Tatar rule in Russia; Ivan III establishes new Russian empire

1481—The Christian Church and the Spanish crown institute the Spanish Inquisition

1487—Southern India's Muslim Bahmani dynasty begins to break up into five independent Muslim kingdoms

1488—Bartholomeu Dias sails around the Cape of Good Hope, Africa's southern tip

1492—Christopher Columbus, sailing for Spain, reaches the Bahamas in the New World; Granada, the last Muslim outpost in Spain, is conquered; Muslims and Jews are driven out of Spain

1494—In the Treaty of Tordesillas, Spain and Portugal divide the New World between them

1497—John Cabot discovers the North American continent, probably at Labrador

1498—Vasco da Gama sails around Africa and reaches India, opening up direct European trade with the Orient; Columbus discovers the South American mainland on his third voyage

1499—Guru Nanak, founder of the Sikh religion, begins preaching; Amerigo Vespucci sails across the Atlantic Ocean to the coast of Venezuela

1500—Pedro Cabral reaches the coast of Brazil and claims it for Portugal; the Amazon River is discovered

1501—Balboa sails with Don Rodrigo de Bastidas to Hispaniola in the New World

1502—Columbus explores the coast of Panama on his fourth voyage

1503—Spain begins slave trade in the New World

1504—French fishermen reach the coast of Newfoundland

1507—Leo Africanus, an Arab, reaches West Africa

1509—Henry VIII becomes king of England

1510—Balboa arrives in present-day Panama

1512—Michelangelo finishes painting his frescoes on the ceiling of Rome's Sistine Chapel; Nicholas Copernicus states that the earth and the other planets revolve around the sun

1513—Italian Prince Machiavelli writes *Il Principe* (*The Prince*), an influential political work; Ponce de Leon discovers Florida; Balboa discovers the South Sea, later named the Pacific Ocean, and claims it for Spain

1514—Pedrarias (Pedro Arias Davila) arrives in Darién as newly appointed governor

1516—Juan de Solis discovers the Rio de la Plata

1517—Protestant Reformation begins when German cleric Martin Luther issues his 95 Theses in Wittenberg, Germany

1519—Ferdinand Magellan begins his voyage to circumnavigate the globe; Ulrich Zwingli begins the Reformation in Zurich, Switzerland; Balboa is executed

Glossary of Terms

ambush—To lie in wait and make a surprise attack

arquebus—A heavy gun whose charge is ignited by a match

baptism—A ceremony of initiation into Christianity by pouring water over the head or immersing the person in water

barnacle—A shellfish that attaches itself to rocks, ships, and other objects in the sea

bicker—To argue

booty—Valuable possessions taken from those conquered in battle

brigantine—A ship with two masts and square sails

broma—A wood-eating worm

caravel—A broad, three-masted sailing ship

cassava—A tropical plant with starchy, edible roots

crossbow—A weapon that hurls a stone or arrow from a bow mounted crosswise

dinghy—A small rowboat

eerie—Strange; weird

exotic—Strange in an attractive or exciting way

fluke—A section of a whale's tail

galleon—A heavy sailing ship used for carrying cargo or waging battles

isthmus—A narrow strip of land between two bodies of water

loot—To take the valuable possessions of conquered people

marooned—Stranded in a place from which there is no escape

notary—An official who draws up documents and makes official records of events

oasis—A moist, fertile spot in an otherwise arid region

quicksilver—A liquid, silver-white form of mercury used in scientific instruments

ramshackle—In poor condition; put together hastily or with poor materials and workmanship

ransack—To search in order to take or steal something

shoal—A shallow place in the water due to built-up sand or soil

stowaway—A person who hides aboard a ship in order to travel on it

thatch—Branches or straw used as a roof

torture—To cruelly inflict pain

treason—The betraying of one's country

Bibliography

For further reading, see:

Anderson, Charles L. G. *Life and Letters of Vasco Núñes de Balboa*. NY: Fleming H. Revell Company, 1946.

Cardini, Franco. *Europe 1492: Portrait of a Continent Five Hundred Years Ago*. NY: Facts on File, 1989.

The Discoverers: The Living Past. NY: Arco Publishing, Inc., 1979.

Hale, John R. *Age of Exploration*. NY: Time-Life Books, 1971.

Herrmann, Paul. *The Great Age of Discovery*. NY: Harper and Brothers, 1958. Translated by Arnold J. Pomerans.

Mirsky, Jeannette. *The Westward Crossings*. NY: Alfred A. Knopf, 1946.

———. *Balboa, Discoverer of the Pacific*. NY: Harper and Row, 1964.

Noble, Iris. *The Honor of Balboa*. NY: Julian Messner, 1970.

Riesenberg, Felix, Jr. *Balboa: Swordsman and Conquistador*. NY: Random House, 1956.

Shore, Maxine and Oblinger, M.M. *Hero of Darién*. NY: Longmans, Green and Co., 1941.

Stefanson, Vilhjalmur. *Great Adventures and Explorations*. NY: The Dial Press, 1947.

Sterne, Emma Gelders. *Vasco Núñez de Balboa*. NY: Alfred A. Knopf, 1961.

Syme, Ronald. *Balboa, Finder of the Pacific*. NY: William Morrow and Company, 1956.

Index

Page numbers in boldface type indicate illustrations.

Picture Identifications for Chapter Opening Spreads

6–7—The Amazon jungle of Ecuador
10–11—Indians at the time of Columbus's arrival in the New World
18–19—Half Moon Bay in Antigua, British West Indies
36–37—The wilds of northern Venezuela
48–49—Frog (*Dendrobates pumilio*) of Panama
60–61—Urubama, Peru
78–79—Ecuadorian jungle at the water's edge
92–93—Panama landscape
108–109—Inca trail in Peru

Acknowledgment

For a critical reading of the manuscript, our thanks to John Parker, Ph.D., Curator, James Ford Bell Library, University of Minnesota, Minneapolis, Minnesota.

Picture Acknowledgements

THE BETTMANN ARCHIVE: 67, 104, 110

H. ARMSTRONG ROBERTS: © M. LANDRE, 105

HISTORICAL PICTURES SERVICE, CHICAGO: 8, 9 14, 15, 22, 25, 26, 47, 66, 69, 71, 74, 75, 77, 82, 90, 91, 97, 99, 102, 103, 107, 111, 112, 116, 117

JIG: © BETTY GROSKIN, 6-7, 60-61, 78-79; © F.E. JENKINS, 18-19; © SAUL MAYER, 57, 92-93

NORTH WIND PICTURE ARCHIVES: 13, 16, 20, 21, 23, 24, 29, 30, 31, 32, 33, 43, 50, 54, 59, 62, 63, 95, 98

CHIP AND ROSA MARIA DE LA CUEVA PETERSON: 4, 101

PHOTRI: 2, 10-11, 41, 106; © HARPERS MONTHLY 1859, 5,53, 56,94

TOM STACK & ASSOCIATES: © ANN & MYRON SUTTON, 36-37, 64; © DAVID G. BAKER, 48-49, 65; © WARREN GARST, 73; © M. TIMOTHY O'KEEFE, 108-109

SUPERSTOCK INTERNATIONAL, INC.: 51, 100

About the Author

Maureen Ash grew up reading books in Milaca, Minnesota. She and her husband raise and work Norwegian Fjord and Suffolk draft horses. They enjoy running, rollerblading, their two small children, and Roy, the family cat.